JANET
JACKSON

JANET JACKSON

Cindy Dyson

CHELSEA HOUSE PUBLISHERS
Philadelphia

Chelsea House Publishers

Editor in Chief	Stephen Reginald
Production Manager	Pamela Loos
Art Director	Sara Davis
Director of Photography	Judy L. Hasday
Managing Editor	James D. Gallagher

Staff for JANET JACKSON

Associate Art Director	Takeshi Takahashi
Design & Production	21st Century Publishing and Communications
Cover Designer	Robert Gerson
Cover photos	AP/Wide World Photos

The Chelsea House World Wide Web address is
http://www.chelseahouse.com

First Printing

1 3 5 7 9 8 6 4 2

Library of Congress Cataloging-in-Publication Data

applied for
ISBN 0-7910-5283-4 (hc)
           0-7910-5284-2 (pb)

Frontis: With albums and singles selling in the millions, Janet Jackson has hit the top of the pop music scene to become one of the most successful entertainers in the world.

CONTENTS

BLACK AMERICANS OF ACHIEVEMENT

HENRY AARON
baseball great

KAREEM ABDUL-JABBAR
basketball great

MUHAMMAD ALI
heavyweight champion

RICHARD ALLEN
religious leader and social activist

MAYA ANGELOU
author

LOUIS ARMSTRONG
musician

ARTHUR ASHE
tennis great

JOSEPHINE BAKER
entertainer

JAMES BALDWIN
author

TYRA BANKS
model

BENJAMIN BANNEKER
scientist and mathematician

COUNT BASIE
bandleader and composer

ANGELA BASSETT
actress

ROMARE BEARDEN
artist

HALLE BERRY
actress

MARY MCLEOD BETHUNE
educator

GEORGE WASHINGTON
CARVER
botanist

JOHNNIE COCHRAN
lawyer

SEAN "PUFFY" COMBS
music producer

BILL COSBY
entertainer

MILES DAVIS
musician

FREDERICK DOUGLASS
abolitionist editor

CHARLES DREW
physician

W. E. B. DU BOIS
scholar and activist

PAUL LAURENCE DUNBAR
poet

DUKE ELLINGTON
bandleader and composer

RALPH ELLISON
author

JULIUS ERVING
basketball great

LOUIS FARRAKHAN
political activist

ELLA FITZGERALD
singer

ARETHA FRANKLIN
entertainer

MORGAN FREEMAN
actor

MARCUS GARVEY
black nationalist leader

JOSH GIBSON
baseball great

WHOOPI GOLDBERG
entertainer

CUBA GOODING JR.
actor

ALEX HALEY
author

PRINCE HALL
social reformer

JIMI HENDRIX
musician

MATTHEW HENSON
explorer

GREGORY HINES
performer

BILLIE HOLIDAY
singer

LENA HORNE
entertainer

WHITNEY HOUSTON
singer and actress

LANGSTON HUGHES
poet

JANET JACKSON
musician

JESSE JACKSON
civil-rights leader and politician

MICHAEL JACKSON
entertainer

SAMUEL L. JACKSON *actor*	JOE LOUIS *heavyweight champion*	ROSA PARKS *civil-rights leader*	TINA TURNER *entertainer*
T. D. JAKES *religious leader*	RONALD MCNAIR *astronaut*	COLIN POWELL *military leader*	ALICE WALKER *author*
JACK JOHNSON *heavyweight champion*	MALCOLM X *militant black leader*	PAUL ROBESON *singer and actor*	MADAM C. J. WALKER *entrepreneur*
MAGIC JOHNSON *basketball great*	BOB MARLEY *musician*	JACKIE ROBINSON *baseball great*	BOOKER T. WASHINGTON *educator*
SCOTT JOPLIN *composer*	THURGOOD MARSHALL *Supreme Court justice*	CHRIS ROCK *comedian and actor*	DENZEL WASHINGTON *actor*
BARBARA JORDAN *politician*	TERRY MCMILLAN *author*	DIANA ROSS *entertainer*	J. C. WATTS *politician*
MICHAEL JORDAN *basketball great*	TONI MORRISON *author*	WILL SMITH *actor*	VANESSA WILLIAMS *singer and actress*
CORETTA SCOTT KING *civil-rights leader*	ELIJAH MUHAMMAD *religious leader*	WESLEY SNIPES *actor*	OPRAH WINFREY *entertainer*
MARTIN LUTHER KING, JR. *civil-rights leader*	EDDIE MURPHY *entertainer*	CLARENCE THOMAS *Supreme Court justice*	TIGER WOODS *golf star*
LEWIS LATIMER *scientist*	JESSE OWENS *champion athlete*	SOJOURNER TRUTH *antislavery activist*	RICHARD WRIGHT *author*
SPIKE LEE *filmmaker*	SATCHEL PAIGE *baseball great*	HARRIET TUBMAN *antislavery activist*	
CARL LEWIS *champion athlete*	CHARLIE PARKER *musician*	NAT TURNER *slave revolt leader*	

ON ACHIEVEMENT

🙚🙚

Coretta Scott King

Before you begin this book, I hope you will ask yourself what the word *excellence* means to you. I think it's a question we should all ask, and keep asking as we grow older and change. Because the truest answer to it should never change. When you think of excellence, perhaps you think of success at work; or of becoming wealthy; or meeting the right person, getting married, and having a good family life.

Those goals are worth striving for, but there is a better way to look at excellence. As Martin Luther King Jr. said in one of his last sermons, "I want you to be first in love. I want you to be first in moral excellence. I want you to be first in generosity. If you want to be important, wonderful. If you want to be great, wonderful. But recognize that he who is greatest among you shall be your servant."

My husband knew that the true meaning of achievement is service. When I met him, in 1952, he was already ordained as a Baptist minister and was working toward a doctoral degree at Boston University. I was studying at the New England Conservatory and dreamed of accomplishments in music. We married a year later, and after I graduated the following year we moved to Montgomery, Alabama. We didn't know it then, but our notions of achievement were about to undergo a dramatic change.

You may have read or heard about what happened next. What began with the boycott of a local bus line grew into a national crusade, and by the time he was assassinated in 1968 my husband had fashioned a black movement powerful enough to shatter forever the practice of racial segregation. What you may not have read about is where he learned to resist injustice without compromising his religious beliefs.

He adopted a strategy of nonviolence from a man of a different race, who lived in a different country and even practiced a different religion. The man was Mahatma Gandhi, the great leader of India, who devoted his life to serving humanity in the spirit of love and nonviolence. It was in these principles that Martin discovered his method for social reform. More than anything else, those two principles were the key to his achievements.

These books are about African Americans who served society through the excellence of their achievements. They form part of the rich history of black men and women in America—a history of stunning accomplishments in every field of human endeavor, from literature and art to science, industry, education, diplomacy, athletics, jurisprudence, even polar exploration.

Not all of the people in this history had the same ideals, but I think you will find that all of them had something in common. Like Martin Luther King Jr., they all decided to become "drum majors" and serve humanity. In that principle—whether it was expressed in books, inventions, or song— they found a goal and a guide outside themselves that showed them a way to serve others instead of living only for themselves.

Reading the stories of these courageous men and women not only helps us discover the principles that we will use to guide our own lives; it also teaches us about our black heritage and about America itself. It is crucial for us to know the heroes and heroines of our history and to realize that the price we paid in our struggle for equality in America was dear. But we must also understand that we have gotten as far as we have partly because America's democratic system and ideals made it possible.

We are still struggling with racism and prejudice. But the great men and women in this series are a tribute to the spirit of the country in which they have flourished. And that makes their stories special and worth knowing.

1

BORN INTO FAME

⚜

A HUGE VIDEO screen featuring a photo of the performer as a baby looms over the stage and the petite singer herself. The audience utters a collective "Awwwww." Janet Jackson's voice rises above the noise of the crowd as she stands before the screen and begins to sing the song "Special" from her latest album, *The Velvet Rope.* "Nothing is more depressing than having everything . . . and still feeling sad," she croons.

The concert is drawing to an end. Janet sings of her struggle to love herself and have confidence in her abilities. Then the music ends abruptly, as she stares into the sea of fans. "Work in progress," she announces, signaling the end of the concert but promising more personal and professional revelations in the future.

Two hours before, a group of Janet's dancers had opened the concert by pulling open the cover of an immense "scrapbook" that actually concealed the video screen. The message: the program would tell the story of the performer's life, a life lived in the glare of media attention.

Like the prop in her concert, Janet Jackson's life has always appeared to be an open book. "Janet may have had specialness thrust upon her; she may even chafe under its demands and restrictions," wrote Vince Aletti of the *Village Voice* in 1997, "but she's

As one of the celebrated Jackson family siblings, performing came naturally to Janet. From her entrance into show business as a child, she has never been out of the spotlight.

11

never not been famous, never not been chosen."

Now in her 30s, Janet Jackson still looks like a teenager. Just under 5' 4" tall, she is slim and muscular. Recently, she's also gone for an edgy look: her hair glows scarlet under stage lights, and her tongue and nose are pierced. A tattoo marks her wrist.

From the time she entered show business as a seven-year-old with chubby cheeks and wide, innocent eyes, Janet has transformed herself time and time again, keeping pace with each new crop of fans she attracts. Today she is one of the most successful entertainers in the world, with a recording contract that is the envy of musicians everywhere. More than 50 million copies of her albums have sold worldwide, including four consecutive multi-platinum records. She has recorded more gold singles than any other female vocalist and also starred in the movie *Poetic Justice*.

Janet is also the "princess" of a family that has been called "America's black royalty"—the famous Jackson family, which includes her siblings Michael, Jermaine, and LaToya, who also remain in America's entertainment spotlight. Janet was just two years old when her five brothers exploded onto the pop music scene as the Jackson Five and propelled her entire family into the public eye. Her most recent incarnation in *The Velvet Rope* is just one more glimpse of a celebrity many followers have known for years. The heart of Janet's appeal, say Ernest Hardy and Natasha Stoval of *Rolling Stone* magazine, is that fans have "paid for the privilege of watching her come into her own. It is a simulated intimacy—but what other kind is there when the object of worship is pure pop product?"

The title of her 1997 album sparked some controversy—some observers initially thought that the term "velvet rope" referred to unconventional sex practices such as bondage. But Janet quickly corrected the misconception. The album is about her inner self, she

A smiling Janet Jackson greets a fan at a New York City music store where she held a CD signing for her 1997 recording The Velvet Rope. Talking about the album, which roused some controversy, Janet has explained that the music and lyrics are an expression of her innermost feelings about her life and experiences as the member of a famous family.

said. She is inviting her listeners to venture past the usual barriers between people and to get to know her better. In a 1997 interview with *Jet* magazine, she explained the title:

> We've all driven by premieres or nightclubs and seen the rope separating those who can enter and those who can't. Well, there's also a velvet rope we have inside us, keeping others from knowing our feelings. In

[this album] I'm trying to expose and explore those feelings. I'm inviting you inside my [barrier]. During my life I've been on both sides of the rope. At times, especially during my childhood, I felt left out and alone. At times I felt misunderstood. . . . But no human heard those feelings expressed. They stayed buried in my past. But [now] the truth has to come out, and for me, the truth takes the form of a song.

"*The Velvet Rope* will mean different things to different people," Janet continued. "To me, it became the concept that allowed me to put into words and music so much of what I've been going through. [It] is my most personal album."

More than most entertainers, Janet has long invested her music with the flavor of her own emotions and experiences. In fact, she believes in using her music both as a kind of cathartic remedy for the pain she has suffered and as a means of celebrating the joy she feels. Janet's music is very much a portrait of Janet herself.

Much of the pain Janet Jackson sings about is the result of surviving a difficult and at times bewildering childhood. The fame of her brothers meant Janet didn't have the chance to experience the normal life of a child growing up in more private circumstances. For her, the most significant source of this pain was her father, Joseph Jackson, who rarely expressed his affection for his children and who drove them, sometimes fiercely, to succeed.

Joseph Jackson was born in Arkansas in 1929 and raised in Tennessee. His own father, a devout Lutheran and a stern schoolteacher, was a strict disciplinarian. Joseph was a teen when his parents divorced, and soon after he dropped out of school to enter Golden Gloves boxing competitions.

Katherine Jackson was her husband's opposite in temperament. A demure, gentle woman, Katherine was born in 1930 and grew up in Alabama. A tolerant, loving parent, she played the clarinet and piano, and she imbued her children with her own love of music.

As a very young child, Katherine had been stricken with polio, a disease that killed many children and left many others severely handicapped. Katherine survived, but until she was a teenager she needed a crutch to help her walk. Her slight limp drew jeers from other children, and even after she no longer needed the crutches she suffered from a lack of self-confidence. A bigger blow came when Katherine's parents divorced when she was 14 years old. Her father had moved his family to East Chicago, Indiana, where he first worked in a steel mill and later as a Pullman porter with the railroad. The split crushed the youngster, who vowed that she would never let such a thing happen in her own life.

Joseph Jackson met Katherine at a party. She fell in love with him at first sight, but Joseph's feelings for her took longer to develop. He had already been married and divorced before he married Katherine in 1949, when she was 18 and he was 21. The newly-weds settled in Gary, Indiana, a town just outside of Chicago that was known for its huge steel manufacturing plants and the smokestacks that dotted the skyline. Small, box-like houses lined the streets where working-class residents, most of them steel mill employees, lived. A high unemployment rate, intense pollution, and a rising crime rate had given Gary the nickname "Sin City." It was not the ideal town in which to raise a family.

Nevertheless Joseph and Katherine settled into a tiny two-bedroom house on Jackson Street, in a predominantly black neighborhood in the heart of town. In 1950 Katherine gave birth to their first child, a girl whom they named Maureen ("Rebbie"). The following year, Sigmund Esco ("Jackie") was born. Two years later another boy, Tariano ("Tito"), arrived. In 1954 the Jacksons had a third son whom they named Jermaine. LaToya, their second daughter,

Spewing smoke and grit, the smokestacks of the U.S. Steel mills characterized the city of Gary, Indiana. When Janet was born there, her father, Joseph, worked in the mills while her mother, Katherine, took a part-time job to support their large family.

was born in 1956, and was followed by three younger brothers: Marlon in 1957, Michael in 1958, and Steven Randall ("Randy") in 1961. And on May 16, 1966, Janet Dameta, the Jacksons' ninth and last child, was born. Katherine recalls that Janet was "a beautiful girl, the most beautiful baby in the entire hospital."

Shortly after Joseph and Katherine had settled

in Gary, Joseph became a crane operator for U.S. Steel, a huge company that paid its laborers relatively good wages for tough, dangerous, and gritty jobs. Katherine took a part-time job with Sears Roebuck & Company, but their two incomes still barely covered the expenses of their large family. At the same time, the Jacksons were constantly on guard to keep their children safe and prevent them from joining the gangs that had sprung up in some of the more dangerous neighborhoods of Gary. Katherine often engaged her children in card and board games, believing that such family activities would help to keep her children off the streets and out of trouble.

As an adult, Janet has expressed great appreciation for the sacrifices her parents—especially her mother—made while the children were growing up. She attributes her own strong work ethic to the lessons she learned as a young girl. "I always think of my mother, whom I adore, and the attitude she expressed: 'Anything to make ends meet,'" Janet told *Rolling Stone* magazine in 1998. "When we lived in Gary, Indiana, when she already had given birth to nine children, she'd walk the winter streets to work at Sears. And this is a woman who, because of polio, walks with pain. This was when my father worked at the steel plant. Work is part of my genetic code; work is in my blood. My response to adversity is always the same: Work harder."

With nine children, the two-bedroom Jackson Street home was quite crowded. Katherine and Joseph shared a bedroom, and all six boys slept in the other bedroom in three bunk beds. The three girls, Rebbie, LaToya, and Janet, slept on a pull-out sofa bed in the living room. The Jacksons went without a telephone for the first few years of their marriage, and their clothing was either homemade or purchased at a local Salvation Army thrift store.

From the start, music was an important element

of family life. Katherine taught each of her daughters to play her favorite instruments. A faithful Jehovah's Witness, Katherine often took her brood to hear the music at her place of worship, the local Kingdom Hall. Joseph too loved music, but his taste was for rhythm-and-blues, and he loved to play his prized electric guitar. He and his brother formed a group called the Falcons, and they performed traditional blues tunes and early rock-and-roll songs by popular artists such as Chuck Berry, Little Richard, and Otis Redding. A disciplined musician, Joseph practiced playing his guitar frequently. On many evenings the Jackson living room was filled with the music of the Falcons rehearsing for their next show.

The Falcons played in clubs and at colleges in and around Chicago, and Joseph was able to take in a little extra cash and enjoy one of his favorite hobbies at the same time. From the beginning, Joseph and Katherine were pleasantly surprised to find that their children quickly took to playing musical instruments and singing along with them. But Joseph didn't realize that his sons prized their father's guitar almost as much as he did. With rapt attention, Tito, Jackie, and Jermaine would watch their father perform, absorbing every chord change and strumming pattern. When Joseph wasn't home, the boys often slipped the guitar out of the closet and secretly practiced playing.

On one of these occasions, the boys broke a guitar string. With no time to replace it before Joseph was due home, they simply put the guitar back in its place and hoped that their father would think the string had broken on its own. Before long, however, Joseph discovered the broken string. Furious that someone had taken out his guitar without permission, he grabbed the instrument and stormed into the boys' bedroom. Tito cringed as Joseph held the guitar over his head. "Let me see what you can do," he growled. Tito was scared, but he took the instrument from his father and began to play.

Joseph was amazed. He believed that his son was not only a good musician, but also that he had the spark of greatness. From that day on, Joseph dedicated himself to seeing that his boys became musical successes. He would do anything to accomplish this goal—pushing and prodding, sometimes screaming at them, to be sure that they practiced regularly and refined their skills. Although Janet had not yet been born, this event held immense importance for her. Joseph Jackson's insight and discipline would propel her older brothers to fame—and their fame would in turn help her launch her own musical career.

Not long after the broken-string incident, Joseph arrived home late from work one day hiding a shiny red guitar, which he had bought for Tito, behind his back. Soon, Jermaine had a bass guitar and an amplifier, and Jackie had maracas. Before long it was difficult to walk through the Jackson living room without tripping over a musical instrument of some kind.

The small house came alive with music night after night. Tito, Jackie, and Joseph played guitars, while Jermaine sang. Rebbie and LaToya played along on the violin and clarinet, while the youngest children, Michael, Randy, and Janet, listened and watched.

Even as a baby, Janet absorbed the rhythms and sounds of the music her family performed. A 1960s tune by Sly and the Family Stone called "Hot Fun in the Summertime" had Janet "jumping up and down" when she was only three years old. "It made me so happy," she told *Rolling Stone* in 1993. "On [my song] 'Woops Now,' I even [use the lyrics], 'I'm out in the sun having fun with my friends' [from that song]. There's also the Turtles' 'Happy

Together' and the Association's 'Windy' and Simon and Garfunkel's 'Feelin' Groovy.' Those [songs] are all precious moments to me. They're about just plain feeling good."

As the Jackson children became more skilled, Joseph became even more demanding. He made them practice for several hours each day and taught them the dance steps he saw popular groups perform. "I helped them when it got hard for them and when they felt disgusted as kids sometimes do . . . when they find it more work than they thought," Joseph said years later. "You have to encourage them to get over that hump."

But by some accounts, Joseph "encouraged" his children to the point that they had little time for any other activities. At times the children trembled as their father criticized their performance or claimed that their dance steps weren't lively enough. Other children sometimes teased the Jacksons about not having the time to play with them. After a while, Rebbie and LaToya grew tired of the demands placed on them, and they dropped out of the family group. They were replaced by Marlon and Michael.

In 1965, a year before Janet was born, Joseph decided that his boys were ready to strut their stuff in front of an audience. They had been practicing seriously for a couple of years by then. Joseph began by entering the boys in local talent contests.

With their practice-perfect vocals and precise dance steps, the boys won several contests. Before long they were making appearances at shopping centers and fund-raising dances. All the while, Joseph kept informed of the latest music trends, making certain that his sons' performances were never out of fashion.

While the Jacksons were earning a name for themselves locally, American popular music was undergoing great changes. In the mid-1960s, British

rock bands like the Beatles and the Rolling Stones were selling record numbers of albums, but black music groups such as the Temptations, the Supremes, and Smokey Robinson and the Miracles were becoming huge successes, attracting large numbers of listeners. Glamour and flash were selling points—

Joseph Jackson demanded that his sons perfect their act. By the early 1970s, the Jackson Five, performing here on The Sonny and Cher Comedy Hour, *were earning acclaim with their trendy pop style.*

performers slicked back their hair, pulled on shiny sharkskin suits, and donned glittering costumes studded with rhinestones and sequins.

Joseph carefully observed these trends. He began to develop a sleek, modern look and sound for his sons that incorporated the classic rhythm-and-blues of his own generation. His boys, he decided, would combine the best of the old with the best of the new. The Jacksons performed as many as 14 shows every weekend, driving for hours between gigs. They'd return home in time for school on Mondays exhausted from their weekends on the road. And after each performance, Joseph gave his boys a detailed critique of their good and bad points.

As the bookings multiplied and the boys earned more money, Joseph went from full-time to part-time at the steel mill so that he could devote more time to managing his boys. He convinced Steeltown, a Gary-based recording label, to sign the Jacksons and produce their first single, "I'm a Big Boy Now," a rhythm-and-blues ballad with call and response vocals between Michael and his brothers. But the song never became a hit.

Janet was just one year old when her brothers got their first big break. In August 1967 the Jacksons were invited to play at the legendary Apollo Theater in the Harlem section of New York City. The Apollo had launched the careers of numerous African-American vocalists and performers. Every Wednesday night the theater held an amateur competition during which the audience decided the winners. The contests were grueling, and the audiences famously showed no mercy: performers who failed to impress Apollo crowds often found themselves pelted with cans and bottles or booed off the stage. But the Jacksons had nothing to fear—they won the competition easily.

And then Motown called.

Motown was one of the most powerful and

influential record companies in the entertainment business. It was also one of the few owned by an African American—Berry Gordy. A songwriter, Gordy had founded Motown out of frustration when he could not find record labels to produce his songs. He created the Motown label in Detroit in 1959, and the company quickly caught up with the biggest New York record companies.

Gordy was renowned for his interest in giving talented unknowns a chance. Many of the people he sponsored went on to become legends in their own right, including Smokey Robinson, Diana Ross, the Temptations, and Stevie Wonder. With his influence, an up-and-coming talent could rise to the top of the charts—but in return Gordy demanded complete control.

Gordy insisted on not only managing the music, dance steps, and costumes of the groups he produced, but also directing all public appearances and even the private lives of his stars. He put his singers through the Motown "charm school," where they were required to learn basic rules of etiquette, proper speech and posture, and methods of conducting successful interviews.

According to the Motown publicity machine, Diana Ross, one of Gordy's singers, discovered the Jacksons and told Gordy about them. Another version of the tale claims that two other singers, Gladys Knight and Bobby Taylor, saw the boys perform and called Motown to alert Gordy to the new talents.

Whatever the true story may be, in 1968 Gordy was certainly looking for a youthful group. Many of the artists he'd groomed in the late 1950s were no longer drawing young record buyers. In the Jacksons, he saw a group that he could mold into a sensation for the next decade. He asked them to come to Detroit for an audition. The Jackson brothers— then ages 17, 14, 13, 11, and 9—won Gordy over.

Two of Motown Records' most famous recording artists, Diana Ross (center) and Smokey Robinson (right), share the spotlight with Motown's founder, Berry Gordy in 1998. Known for spotting talent, Gordy immediately saw the potential of the Jackson brothers and signed them on for their recording debut.

He loved them.

"I'm going to make you the biggest thing in the world, and you're gonna be written about in history books," Gordy told the boys. "Your first record will be a number one, your second record will be a number one, and so will your third record. Three number one records in a row. You'll hit the charts just as Diana Ross and the Supremes did."

At the time, Berry Gordy was in the process of

moving Motown's headquarters from Detroit, Michigan, to Los Angeles, California. His goal was to tackle filmmaking in the same way he had tackled record-making. And because he had just signed on the Jacksons, he said, they would have to move west with him.

2

GROWING UP JANET

❧

JANET JACKSON WAS only two years old when her father and brothers moved to Los Angeles. She stayed behind with her mother, LaToya, Rebbie, and the youngest Jackson son, Randy, while Joseph traveled to California with the other children. The rest of the family would not move for another 18 months.

The Jackson boys, who were now known professionally as the Jackson Five, were tended to not only by Joseph but also by Berry Gordy and by Diana Ross. Both Gordy and Ross lived on the same Beverly Hills street, and they often took turns watching the boys.

The Jackson Five's rise to fame began with intensive preparation. Just as he had done for his other performers, Gordy carefully taught the boys how to dress and how to behave in the presence of the media. He wanted to make sure his singing stars acted like gentlemen. He also wanted to make sure they had style: each of the boys was given a trendy "Afro" hairstyle and a closet full of fashionable clothing in psychedelic patterns and colors.

The Jackson Five made their recording debut on the coattails of Diana Ross's fame with the release of the album *Diana Ross Presents the Jackson Five*. They were an immediate hit. Their first single, "I Want You Back," was released in November 1969 and sold two million copies in six weeks. The song quickly shot to number one on the pop music charts. Their second,

When Janet was growing up, she was overshadowed by the attention showered on her brothers. The Jackson 5 (from left to right, Tito, Marlon, Michael, Jackie, and Jermaine) recorded, toured, appeared on numerous TV shows and magazine covers, and were idolized by teenagers nationwide.

third, and fourth singles also reached number one—a record that marked the first time that a group so young had made such a big splash in the music industry.

Suddenly the Jackson Five was a media sensation. The group was invited to appear on the *Ed Sullivan Show*, the *Tonight Show*, *American Bandstand*, and *Soul Train*. The boys were featured on the covers of several major magazines. They embarked on a national tour and collected numerous music awards; everywhere they went, gaggles of enthralled teenage girls clamored for them. Steve Manning, who answered fan mail for the Jackson Five, recalls that the group was a smash hit primarily because it struck a chord in a country that was developing a growing awareness of the rich heritage of African Americans. "The Jackson Five then [was] a very timely group for black Americans," Manning remembers. "It was the time of the Afro and black pride. Never before had black teenagers had someone to idolize like that."

The Jackson Five became so famous that they inspired a children's television show. In the summer of 1971, a weekly cartoon series debuted that featured characters modeled after the five brothers. For Janet, still living with her mother and separated from her older siblings, the series provided a way to feel closer to her brothers. "I absolutely loved those cartoons," Janet recalled in 1998. She continued:

> I was amazed to see my brothers as these lovable cartoon characters. It made me love them and miss them even more. . . . It also gave me a feeling that everything was all right. Cartoon characters don't have real problems. I guess I wanted to join them and become a cartoon character myself. I was a kid who found it easier telling my problem to animals than to real people.

Already, Janet had begun to experience the loneliness that came with being a member of a famous family. While still a toddler, she felt estranged from

her distant, disapproving father, an emotion that would plague her throughout her childhood.

Despite the Jackson brothers' fame, Joseph and Katherine wanted their children to lead lives that were as normal as possible. By now the family had moved into a spacious home in California and had a comfortable income. But Joseph did not want his children to take their good fortune for granted, and he continued to treat his children sternly.

The children were denied their regular allowances if they did not complete homework assignments or if they did not work hard enough at school or in rehearsals. None of them were allowed out past

Feeling emotionally distant from her stern and demanding father, Janet had a warm relationship with her mother (shown here in a happy moment with Janet). Although Katherine, like Joseph, believed in discipline for her children, it was she who played games and had fun with them.

9 P.M., and the children were forbidden to go on dates until they had reached 12th grade. The Jacksons had a housekeeper and a cook, but each child was still required to do specific chores. Phone calls were limited to five minutes. "If you can't say what you need to in that time, you'd better sit down and think about what you're calling about before you use the phone," Joseph used to say.

But the Jackson children also found time to pursue their own interests. Saturdays were fun days. They were allowed to invite friends over to watch movies, dance, or play with family pets. "It was like a big carnival," Janet's sister LaToya recalled.

Joseph and Katherine tried to keep their children at home as often as possible to protect them from outsiders and publicity seekers. But some of the children, including Janet, began to feel isolated. "I was sheltered," Janet said, "and there's good and bad to that. The good was not getting into the drugs and the alcohol. . . . The bad was finally coming out into the real world and trying to deal with it, which was hard for me." For example, Janet did not learn to drive until she was well past legal age, in part out of fear. In 1981 her brother Randy was badly injured in a car accident and required months of physical therapy before he could walk again. Afraid to try driving herself after her brother's mishap, Janet instead was able to let a chauffeur take her where she needed to go.

In 1971 Joseph and Katherine had bought a two-acre estate on Hayvenhurst Avenue in Encino, California, a wealthy suburb in the San Fernando Valley. The Tudor-style mansion with stucco walls and dark beams earned a reputation as being a kind of fairy-tale dwelling. A tea room was decorated with figurines of Snow White and the Seven Dwarfs, and the home included a movie theater, a photography darkroom, a recording studio, a gym and sauna, and a trophy room filled with awards that the Jackson Five had won. A full-size basketball court had been built on the estate grounds, which were dotted with orange trees. The compound was surrounded by a security fence and monitored by closed-circuit television cameras.

The security measures were not unwarranted. "There was always so much stuff going on," Janet remembered:

> There were girls we didn't know wanting to come over and visit [my brothers]. There were interviews, television cameras all the time, people screaming, concerts, photo sessions. I mean, it wasn't what you'd call a normal household, let's face it. My brothers were teen idols, and sometimes we got sick of it. We had to have our phone number changed maybe once a week. And then these girls would still call. Who knows how they got the number? LaToya and I used to laugh because they made such fools of themselves over our brothers. And to us, well, they were just our noisy, smelly brothers.

Even as a young girl, though, Janet knew that she wanted to be a star like her siblings. Their success was "inspiring," she said. "I knew at an early age I wanted to be an entertainer, but I didn't know how I would ever go about such a thing. I just knew that if they could do it, maybe I had a chance, too. Every little girl wants to be a star. . . . I thought just maybe I had a better edge than most other little girls."

Janet enjoyed riding horses, swimming, and playing music with her brothers more than she liked shopping or other interests she shared with her sisters. "I used to wear nothing but blue jeans, T-shirts and gym shorts," Janet said. "Before [my teens] you couldn't get me in a dress. . . . I used to always sit with my legs up and my mom would always say, 'Janet, put your legs down.' You can't be free in a dress."

The Jacksons kept a virtual zoo of exotic animals, including a llama named Lola, a deer, and a giraffe. At various times during Janet's youth, the Jackson home housed a chimpanzee, several swans, a white

Janet, cuddling a baby bear, has never lost her love for animals. For her, the pets in the Jackson household were friends with whom she could share her loneliness and who helped her cope with the isolation she often felt as a child.

peacock, cockatoos, parrots, and even a boa constrictor named Muscles, whom Michael brought home after Janet displayed an interest in snakes. The animals at the Jackson mansion were more than pets to Janet, however. They were childhood "friends" who helped her get over her loneliness and insecurities:

> I was very independent growing up, but there were things that were bothering me that I never told anybody. I would talk to our animals at home. We had fawns that Michael and I raised until we weaned them and we'd feed them every morning. And I would talk to them. . . . I felt they understood me. We had four dogs, and I would climb in the bushes and sit down and speak with them. . . . And that's how I dealt with [my life] in the very, very beginning, when I was a kid.

Janet even took to letting Muscles sleep with her. "My mom called me crazy that I would let him sleep on my headboard," Janet said. "But I trusted him from the start." And though the family had many dogs throughout Janet's pre-teen years, her favorite was Fluffy, a mixed poodle-terrier that she took home after finding it in a nearby park. Janet also loved horses—so much so that she considered becoming a jockey.

While they were growing up, Michael was Janet's favorite brother. When he wasn't on tour with the band, she followed him everywhere. Of her eight siblings, she felt that she had the most in common with Michael, and the two spent hours together. In the mornings Michael often woke her up at 6 A.M. just so they could talk. "He [would] knock on my door and say, 'Dunk, are you up?'" Janet recalled. "I [would] tell him, 'No, but come in anyway.'" (Janet's nickname, "Dunk," was coined to describe her sturdy body, which Michael claimed resembled a donkey.)

By outward appearances, Janet's childhood after her brothers' rise to fame seems to have been charmed. But it was not what it seemed. "My own home life was tense," Janet said. "We'd be in bed with our mother, playing games, having fun, and when we saw the reflection of the lights of [my father's] car pulling up the driveway, we'd scatter to our rooms," she told a *Rolling Stone* interviewer in 1993. "There was a coldness, a detachment about our father, that was chilling. We'd all learn from his discipline, but I believe we suffered because he wasn't there for us emotionally." Several years later, Janet explained that she still feels that distance from her father. "It hasn't gotten any better," she said in 1997. "Because he wouldn't allow me to be [close to him]—and still won't. It's as simple as that. That's just the way he is."

Janet remembers the day her father told her to stop calling him Dad. "I will never forget that," says Janet. "I was really young, about 6 or 7, and as a kid,

Janet gets a hug and kiss from brother Michael. Of her brothers, Janet has been closest to Michael from the time she was a child. The two spent as much time together as possible talking and sharing their common love for animals.

that was very hurtful to me." From that day on, Janet called her father Joseph. "I went through a lot, from age 15 to about 19 years," Janet says. "I was very young. I used to hurt so badly that I'd ask God why, what have I done to deserve this?"

In addition to her difficult relationship with her father, Janet also experienced the normal growing pains of most teenagers. At 14, she felt that she was too heavy; her brothers teased her for her chunky figure. Like Michael, she had already given up red meat some years earlier, believing that it would help her take off the extra pounds. But it didn't work.

Both Jacksons also resorted to another way of changing their looks. Michael had had the first Jackson family "makeover" when, at 14, he had his nose altered by plastic surgery. Janet asked her parents if she could get her nose narrowed as well, and they didn't see any harm in it. In fact, they seemed to think that anything that would help further their children's careers was worth doing. Unfortunately, even after a second plastic surgery a few years later, Janet remained surprisingly displeased with her looks. "Want to know what I see when I look in the mirror?" Janet asked an interviewer in 1994. "Well, I'll tell you. I see too much face. Look at these jaws. No matter how thin I might get, my face will always look big because I inherited these jaws from my grandmother."

In later years, the surgeries both she and Michael underwent would lead to accusations that they were altering their looks in an attempt to look more "white." Janet dismissed the criticism. "I look in the mirror and I know who I am. I know I'm black," Janet said. "And I'm proud of that."

3

HELLO SHOW BUSINESS

·◖◗·

Seven-year-old Janet (fore-ground) was already a seasoned performer when she joined her siblings on the CBS television variety show The Jacksons *in 1976. Randy stands behind Janet and next to LaToya and Rebbie. From left to right in the back are Jackie, Michael, Tito, and Marlon. The Jacksons were the first black family to have starring roles in a television series.*

WHILE THE JACKSON brothers were earning their claims to fame, Janet sometimes traveled with the tour. The Jackson Five had truly become a family act: Joseph managed the group, while Katherine created costumes and made sure all of her children were well fed and cared for.

After she first went on tour with her brothers, Janet began thinking of ways to join the act. Katherine encouraged Janet to improve her vocal skills by practicing scales and singing short songs. Together mother and daughter listened to a broad variety of musical styles so that Janet could get a feel for each one. Janet loved to imitate the voices she heard, and when she first listened to Mae West—a brash movie star of the 1930s who was famous for her sultry, brusque style—Janet found a voice she loved. Joseph heard her imitations, and he decided that it was time for Janet join the family show.

"He knew I could do it, I guess," Janet remembered. "He knew a lot more than I did, or than I wanted to admit. I was always so shy, I couldn't imagine getting up on stage and performing. But I knew inside that this was what I really wanted to do. If it wasn't for my father though, I would never have been able to get up on that stage."

To prepare for her debut, Janet practiced endlessly, rehearsing with her brothers every day and working with a tutor to make up for the time she wasn't attending school. Michael worked especially hard to help his sister. "Put more into it," he would say, encouraging her to express her emotions in her music. "Show the way you feel!"

In 1973 the youngest Jackson child, just seven years old, joined the family act along with her brother Randy. The family was scheduled to perform at the ritzy MGM Grand Hotel in Las Vegas, Nevada —a venue that could make or break careers. It was important that all the Jacksons be in top shape and primed to perform. Janet had better be good.

The little girl's heart pounded as she waited to go onstage. Her eyes met her 12-year-old brother Randy's as if looking for courage. "Don't worry," he whispered. "I know you'll be good." Then Michael announced Janet and Randy to the crowd. Little Janet, dressed in a backless pink satin gown and festooned with a matching feather boa, strutted into the spotlight wearing a huge smile. A small ripple of applause skipped through the audience. Janet smacked her hand to her hip and said, "How ya' doin' big boy?" in her best Mae West imitation. The audience rocked with laughter.

By the time the skit ended, Janet had won over the crowd. She rushed from the stage, knowing that she had done a great job. The brief stage appearance launched her show-business career.

Before long, Janet and Randy were appearing regularly in the family's Las Vegas performances. "My father put everyone in the act, and my brother Randy and I were doing impressions of everyone from Jeanette MacDonald and Nelson Eddy to Mickey and Sylvia," Janet said. "We sang 'Love Is Strange,' and I was dancing my little butt off, throwing my hips to the beat of the drum."

Two years later, CBS invited the Jackson family to bring their act to television. This was no animated cartoon series, however; it was a showcase series

Part of The Jacksons *show included skits like this in which Janet displayed her acting talent. With broom and blonde wig, she appeared as Cinderella opposite guest star Betty White, who played the fairy godmother.*

featuring the Jacksons themselves.

The premiere of *The Jacksons* in 1976 marked the first time a black family had ever starred in a television series. After their opening song, "Forever Came Today," Michael introduced the family act. "We're the Jacksons," he announced. "All of you who were expecting the Osmonds [a white family of performers, featuring siblings Donny and Marie], do not adjust the color of your set," he joked. He then introduced the members he called "the sexy side of the family": his sisters Rebbie and LaToya. "Okay, let's go,"

Michael yelled out as the family prepared to reprise their opening number.

"Hold it right there, dude!" came a voice from offstage.

Nine-year-old Janet stomped onto the stage wearing a long blue skirt and matching boots, her thick hair pulled back into a little puff. "Nothing goes 'til I say it goes," she announced with mock attitude.

"Oh, I forgot," Michael joked. "This is our little sister, Janet Jackson."

After applause, Janet announced, "That's right. I'm Janet Jackson and nothing goes until I say, 'go.'"

"Okay," she announced after a brief pause, snapping her fingers, "go."

The show was a hit, and Janet, not yet 10 years old, was on her way to stardom. A television producer named Norman Lear saw her perform on one episode of *The Jacksons* and decided to recruit her for a part in a family-style TV comedy called *Good Times*. Like the Jacksons's variety show, this program was one of the first to feature a black family as main characters.

Lear knew right away that he had the right girl for the job. Before Janet read the script, he asked whether she knew how to cry on cue. Janet said she thought she could, so Lear gave her a scenario: she had just given him a tie he didn't like. He said some mean things about the tie and about her. On cue, Janet began to cry. "You've got the job," Lear declared.

"There was a pain deep inside I could get to quickly, even as a little girl," Janet said, explaining her ability to cry. Janet was cast as Penny Gordon, the child of foster parents who had been physically abused by her birth mother. For two years, from 1977 to 1979, Janet played Penny Gordon.

Now a pre-teen, Janet was on her own for several hours each day for the first time in her life. She began to love the feeling of independence from her family.

"I was by myself," Janet remembers. "But the cast made me feel so welcome that it became my second family." Crew members and fellow actors on the set of *Good Times* remember Janet as extremely shy, rarely chatting or joking with them, but working hard.

When *Good Times* was canceled, Janet, then 14, took another acting role—as Charlene, the girlfriend of Willis (Todd Bridges) on *Diff'rent Strokes*. The show drew good ratings, and Janet's sense of fashion

Janet became a star in her own right when she got the role of foster child Penny Gordon on the television sitcom Good Times. *Here, she plays a scene with comedian Jimmy Walker in a 1977 episode.*

influenced teens across the country, who began copying her layered hairstyle and wearing hoop earrings just as she did.

On the set, Janet remained shy but very professional. "I was very embarrassed when I had to do romantic scenes with Todd," Janet said at the time. "But you just have to block all that out. I socialize with Todd sometimes. We talk a lot on the phone, and sometimes we go to movies. Todd is a sweetheart." To rumors that she and Todd were dating in real life, Janet responded "We're just good friends."

In a magazine interview, Janet tried to explain the differences between her television character and herself. "In some ways, Janet and Charlene are the same," she said, "but the difference is [that Charlene] comes out and says whatever she has to, and I can't. [My TV character] shows her feelings, but if I'm upset and angry, I just can't come right out and tell the person. It takes me quite a while. That's the main difference. She speaks up and I don't."

Until seventh grade, Janet spent a great deal of time on the road and was therefore tutored regularly rather than attending public school. She has fond memories of her favorite tutor, Rose Fine. Mrs. Fine was accredited by the state of California as a children's welfare supervisor and became not only a teacher but also a kind of second mother for Janet and her brothers while they were on the road. "On certain days, I felt like the luckiest kid in the world," Janet said. "Not only was my own mother great, but we had . . . Mrs. Fine. . . . [She] would travel with us and hold class in our hotel room. You can't realize how comforting, how wonderful it was to go to school with all my brothers and sisters. When we had a problem we wouldn't want our mother to know about, we went to Mrs. Fine."

When the family wasn't traveling, Janet attended public school, but she didn't enjoy it as much as being tutored. Always the "new kid," Janet was shy and had

Janet and costar Todd Bridges in a scene from Diff'rent Strokes. Janet's popularity as an actor soared among other teens when she played Todd's outspoken girlfriend, Charlene, in the hit television comedy.

trouble making friends. "I was a part of something very wonderful," Janet said, talking about her family's fame, "and yet [I] felt cut off. I remember watching a troop of Girl Scouts, thinking how great it would be to join, knowing I couldn't because I had already started traveling and entertaining. The simplest things—like having a close friend—seemed beyond my grasp."

For many years, Janet relied mainly on brother Michael for friendship. In many ways he was a typical brother, teasing Janet whenever he got the chance. Once after Janet had seen the movie *Jaws*, she was afraid to go into the family swimming pool, so Michael offered to go with her and protect her from any sharks that managed to get into the pool. Instead, he dove underwater and grabbed her leg. Needless to say, she screamed.

Ironically, her brothers' fame made it more difficult to find real friends. "You didn't know who was your friend for you," she said. "I had friends coming to my house for the first time and bringing a present for my brothers. They're my friend, and they've never given me a present."

While she remained in public school, she did find companions among the black students who had been bused from the rough area of South Central Los Angeles into the predominantly white neighborhood. "At lunch time, the black kids would stick together and dance like crazy," Janet remembered. "I gravitated over to the black kids. I enjoyed being in the middle of the action. I felt at home. I'd have my mother drive me over the hill [to South Central] so I could visit my friends."

"I used to see kids like that and envy them," Janet would say years later. "I was a tomboy, and I guess I wanted to run a little wild, feel free, be normal. Coming over here [to South Central Los Angeles from a wealthier part of the city], I got a glimpse of a world that seemed a lot more natural to me. . . .

I felt welcome here."

Away from the comfortable circle of her siblings and Mrs. Fine, Janet also felt overcome by the lessons she was required to learn. Today, Janet attributes her later bouts with depression in part to these early experiences at school:

> Some of my teachers weren't nice to me. I remember when I got my first black teacher. I was in the fourth grade. Mrs. Womack. And I thought she was the most beautiful thing. And she was such a sweet lady and so kind to me. Not all my Caucasian [white] teachers were mean, but I had a couple that weren't nice to me at all. One of them embarrassed me in front of the entire class, and I just never got over that. . . .
>
> I was supposed to do some equation on the board, and I couldn't figure it out. And she was like, "Think, Jackson! Use your head! Oh, God, this is so simple!" It made me feel very stupid, and it hurt me so much. . . . I felt not deserving, not good enough. Like, why do I deserve to have success? I'm not a smart person. You know what I mean? And the thing is, that's still the way I feel about myself sometimes.

By the seventh grade, Janet had become too famous from her *Good Times* role to comfortably attend public school. "Kids would run after me and look up to me in an embarrassing way," Janet remembered. "They'd say 'Don't do this or that around her; she's a star.' I'd explain, 'Television, that's my work—I'm just the same as you; we're equal.'" Janet transferred to Valley Professional School, an institution where most kids were also entertainers or actors. She was surrounded by musicians, dancers, and actors who were dedicated to learning how to improve their skills and become successful entertainers. But even there, she sometimes had trouble relating to other kids her age. She saw many of them as rich and spoiled. "You turned sixteen and you'd get a Porsche for your birthday," Janet said of her classmates. "Or some kid would drive up in her Mercedes. It was like *Beverly Hills 90210*. In my family . . . if you wanted a car, you had to buy your own. But we couldn't buy one until we were eighteen."

Although she toyed with the idea of going to college and getting a degree in business, by the time she graduated from Valley Professional in 1984, Janet had decided that performing onstage seemed like the best career choice.

Despite all the fame, Janet had remained a shy girl, especially when it came to singing. She didn't enjoy "competing" with her brothers and sisters. One day LaToya, who had a moderately successful singing career, was working in the family recording studio, and Janet stopped by to watch. At one point, Janet, who was still in school at the time, thought the song's arrangement didn't sound quite right. For the first time, she piped up. "This is how the sound should go," she told LaToya, and then she sang an example of what she had in mind.

LaToya liked what she heard and taped her younger sister singing. When Janet's parents heard the tape, they were amazed. "My father asked if I would like to start singing again," Janet recalled. "I never saw myself as a solo artist like my brothers and sisters. Do you think I'm ready?" she asked. "What if people don't like my voice?" "Believe me," he answered, "you're ready."

The turning point for Janet came in 1981, when she and her sisters, Rebbie and LaToya, decided to form their own female version of the Jackson Five. Unfortunately they were unsuccessful, in part because they had great trouble cooperating with one another. "Janet made a decision that would have personal and professional consequences more far-reaching than she could possibly have imagined at the time," biographer Bart Andrews commented in 1994. "'All right,' she concluded, 'I'm just going to have to make it by myself.' It was a fateful moment. The thought was to echo in her mind again and again. 'I'll do it on my own.'"

In 1982, at 15 years old, Janet signed a contract with A&M Records, with her father Joseph as her manager. Her first album, *Janet Jackson*, a pop record incorporating rhythm-and-blues touches, sold 250,000 copies. Her second album, *Dream Street*, was released in 1984—the same year she took another acting role, as a young student attending a performing arts school in the television series *Fame*, which was modeled after the 1980 movie of the same name.

Janet's first two recording ventures were disappointing. Critics panned them as sugar-coated pop, and they criticized Janet's wispy voice. Some claimed that the only reason she was able to record them at all was because of the fame of her brother, Michael, who by now had earned a name for himself as a solo performer.

"On my first album the songs were sort of teenage-like," Janet admitted. "I wanted to make a change in my second album. The first album introduces you. The second one sets your image. I couldn't stay like that. People would still look at me as a little girl and I'd never grow."

Among the promotions Janet embarked on was a tour of American high schools, during which she acted as a spokesperson for a program called Commitment to Education. "I really feel the kids listened to what I was saying," Janet said. "I'd tell them about my family and about how a good education gives you the ability to get a job."

Although her records weren't big hits, they did much to publicize the performer's singing career. Already she was attracting some fanatical admirers. Janet remembers appearing at one high school where a student got so excited to see her that the student pulled her hair. And at 17, Janet seemed ready to break out and do something big. "There's another

*Enthusiastic fans greet a
Michael Jackson concert. As
Janet began her recording career,
Michael left his brothers and
burst upon the pop music world
as a solo performer, launching
a career that made him a world-
famous musical artist.*

lady inside Janet who's getting ready to come out,"
predicted Jeryl Busby, a record executive at A&M.
"I think she could be the biggest star in the family."

While Janet was still finishing high school and
making her first forays into recording, brother
Michael was taking the pop music scene by storm.
In 1979 he had left his brothers and found a new
manager in an effort to strike out on his own. He was
21 and itching for more control of his music. Hooking
up with the legendary music producer Quincy Jones
proved to be Michael's most important and far-
reaching decision. The first album produced by the

two, *Off the Wall,* was a blockbuster hit. In 1981 Michael began work on another album, which he ultimately titled *Thriller.*

This second solo effort would cement Michael's place as the most successful musical entertainer in the world. The album broke several sales records and earned eight Grammy awards. In addition, Michael spent $1.2 million creating a music video as a showpiece for the title track. The piece transformed the music video from a promotional tool to an art form and made history.

4

OUT OF THE
FAMILY'S SHADOW

❧

I N 1984, AT 18 years old, Janet Jackson eloped
with James DeBarge, 21, a member of another successful singing family. She'd known James for a long
time: they had met when she was 13 years old at a
Detroit recording studio, and the two had kept in
touch over the years. By the time Janet turned 16, she
had become enamored of him and the two began
sneaking off together, avoiding the strict rules of the
Jackson family that prohibited dating before age 18.

Katherine and Joseph were not pleased with
James, but the more they tried to keep Janet from seeing him the more determined she became to maintain
a relationship with him. On September 7, 1984, the
couple was married in a private church ceremony in
James's hometown of Grand Rapids, Michigan.

But the marriage was difficult from the very first
night. According to biographer Bart Andrews, after
the newlyweds checked into an expensive hotel suite
in Grand Rapids, James went out to visit friends and
left Janet alone. When he returned he was clearly
drunk. "Janet was waiting up for me with tears stream-
ing down her face," James later recalled.

Janet and James's marriage lasted about a year.
Publicly Janet said that she'd had the marriage
annulled because their careers left the couple with
little time for themselves. But according to Bart
Andrews, James had a drug problem that crippled the

*From the heartache of her
failed marriage to singer James
DeBarge (shown here with
Janet in 1986), Janet gained
the strength to leave the shadow
of her family and pursue her
own dream of becoming a
recording star.*

union. "You always think you can change people,"
Janet admitted later. "And I knew he wanted to
change so badly. He was trying—but he wasn't trying
hard enough."

Eventually Janet began to realize that she couldn't
help James. "God, I felt like my whole life was falling
down," she said. "And I could see him going down,
but there was nothing I could do. And James said
to me, 'Well, you haven't tried to help me,' but
I thought, 'What about helping yourself, too?' I felt
myself going down with him and I thought, 'I can
either go down with him and that's the end of my life,
or I can just let go and continue on by myself.'" On
January 7, 1985, a sadder and wiser Janet left James.
They were granted an annulment on November 18,
1985.

In the midst of anguish and regret, Janet also realized that she had become a stronger, more resilient
person. "I survived really tough times," she has said
about that period of her life. "It amazed me. I didn't
know I was that strong. I just never dreamed it. I'd be
surprised if I ever again go as low as I did during that
period."

Janet believes her early concept of marriage must
have been influenced by the rocky relationship
between her parents. Katherine had threatened to
leave Joseph Jackson at least twice because of his affairs
with other women. In 1973 she filed for divorce, but
she allowed Joseph to continue living at home and
eventually dropped the legal proceedings. Joseph's
string of affairs resumed, and each time he seemed to
grow less concerned about being found out. In 1982
Katherine filed again, but once more she allowed
Joseph to stay on until the paperwork was final.

Fortunately Janet found consolation from the
heartache of her breakup with James DeBarge. She
began to rely on a trusted friend, Rene Elizondo,
whom she had known for several years. Rene's parents had moved with him from Mexico to the San

Fernando Valley when he was a child. A mutual friend had introduced him to Janet after Michael Jackson had seen Rene in a dance performance. Michael invited Rene to the Jackson house, and he and Janet became fast friends.

"When I first met him I was going through so much, and I would call him, and I would cry on the phone," Janet said. "And he was going through some stuff too, with his girlfriend. We were best friends. Then, when I was about 20, it was the strangest thing when we started being attracted to each other. . . . It might sound strange, but we were such good friends. But I think those are the best relationships, when you are friends first."

One writer described Rene as having the demeanor of a Latin aristocrat. At his core, Rene is a dancer, but he also enjoys filmmaking, songwriting, and photography. He's an extrovert, eager and willing to meet problems and opportunities head on. His sense of humor has been described as quirky. Janet came to admire him for his outgoing personality and vitality, while Rene developed great respect for Janet's honesty and courage.

By the time Janet was 20, the relationship between Rene and Janet had evolved and deepened. The two fell in love. Observers of the couple commented on their easy rapport and sense of playfulness. "When I've watched Janet and Rene work together in the studio or discuss matters in their Malibu home, they appear as two halves of a whole," wrote David Ritz in *Rolling Stone*. "They're both lightning-fast thinkers, and one often completes a thought the other has begun. There seems to be no hierarchy, no boss. They operate on the same wavelength. They're almost always together, and Rene, as chief adviser and constant collaborator, is intensely focused on Janet's career."

In the midst of her breakup with James DeBarge, Janet managed to turn misfortune and heartache into

After the breakup of her marriage, Janet found the love and security she needed in her relationship with Rene Elizondo. As Janet's close adviser and collaborator, Rene watched over and guided her career throughout the 1980s and '90s.

music by creating her first widely acclaimed album, *Control*. By the mid-1980s, the wide appeal of music videos had revolutionized the popular music scene. Personal style and dance became as important in selling a song as the music itself. To make a hit, an entertainer also needed to become a hot item on music video TV channels such as MTV and VH1. And, in order to be a hot MTV item, an entertainer had to have a cultivated, individual "look."

Janet knew that she had to buckle down and work hard to compete in the industry. She began taking voice and dance lessons, and at the urging of a trusted executive at A&M Records she went to a weight clinic to slim down. The transformation was just what

Janet needed. "It seems difficult to imagine that back in 1985 most people perceived [Janet] as just another one of the more incidental Jackson kids, one with marginal talent," Andrews comments. "Indeed, Janet was thought of as nothing more than Michael's little sister, a sometimes convincing actress, half-decent dancer and barely adequate singer."

Janet made a crucial move that would change that perception and set her on the path to stardom. She hooked up with Jimmy "Jam" Harris and Terry Lewis, former members of the Time, an all-black group whose members were protégés of the legendary recording artist formerly named Prince. "I told them my whole story, what I wanted to do," Janet said. "I said, 'I need you guys to help me express how I feel, to help me get my feelings out.'" Struggling to make a name for themselves as songwriters and record producers, Harris and Lewis were eager to take a chance on Janet.

"When I've made records in the past, I've usually been given a tape of a song, learned it, and then go into the studio and sung to a completed instrumental track," Janet said. "This time around, I intended to be completely involved in the recording process, from the song writing to the playing to the production." Janet wanted her third album to be her anthem of independence. Fittingly, she named it *Control*. "I'm just taking control of my life," Janet said. "That's what the album is about—control—and I've got lots of it."

The album's first single, "What Have You Done for Me Lately?" was released in January 1986 and quickly rose to number one. The self that Janet had exposed in her new album was very different than the public's image of the cute, sweet, shy younger sister to the Jackson brothers. The change was so striking that even Janet's mother, Katherine, wasn't quite sure that she liked this new persona of her daughter's.

Janet explained that the lyrics of *Control* reflect

feelings and thoughts she has experienced. It marked what would become Janet's trademark style—solidifying her own feelings in her music. "*Control* was an album about what I went through in my life from ages 16 to 19, and the self-discovery that resulted," Janet said. In one of the hit songs, "Nasty," Janet demands respect from those who see her as a young innocent: "No, my name ain't baby—it's Janet," she declares, "Miss Jackson if you're nasty." In another of the song's lyrics, she sings: "I'm not a prude. I just want some respect. 'Cause privacy is my middle name."

The album quickly made Janet a role model for teens and young women who wanted to take charge of their own lives, to live their own dreams. "Janet's young followers had never really seen this type of hard-bitten attitude from a young, female R&B act let alone a Jackson," biographer Andrews wrote. "Before *Control*, female confidence like this prevailed only among 'old school' R&B artists. . . . Between Jackson's sauciness and beauty, and Harris and Lewis' irresistible beat, the public was immediately intoxicated by practically everything on *Control*."

Control stole the critics' hearts and stayed at number one on the charts for four consecutive weeks. In 1987 the album was nominated for nine American Music Awards—more than any other album or performer—and it earned Janet Jackson the award for Favorite Soul Single and Favorite Female Video Artist in the Soul, Rhythm-and-Blues category. Janet also performed a number from *Control* for the awards ceremony audience. The album also received three Grammy award nominations that year: Album of the Year, Best Vocal Female, and Best Song (for "What Have You Done for Me Lately?").

The Jackson family now included two superstars, and home life at the Encino mansion become even more quirky and restricted. At times family members felt like prisoners, forced to remain behind the gates and security guards that kept overenthusiastic fans

out. But once in a while someone sneaked through.

"Once, I was at the front gate when Janet came racing up the drive in her car from the outside, through the open gate, and up to the house at what seemed like a hundred miles an hour," recalled a former guard for the Jacksons. "She hit the brakes so hard when she reached the end of the driveway, we thought she must have hurt herself. Three of us raced to the car. Inside, Janet was sitting at the wheel, crying, babbling that someone was after her. 'He's been following me,' she said. 'He's after me.' . . . Janet didn't leave the house after that for about a week."

Seeking a more normal life and a measure of independence, in late 1987 Janet decided to move out of

The talents of producers Jimmy "Jam" Harris (left) and Terry Lewis helped make Janet's third album, Control, *a huge success.* Control *made her a superstar and garnered numerous prestigious awards. The title, she explained, reflected her newfound independence and her ability to run her own life.*

the mansion and into her own place with Rene. At the same time Janet decided to drop her father as her manager. He had not been a part of her success with *Control*. In fact he had advised her not to hire Harris and Lewis, and he was strongly critical of the end product. "I remember trying to tell my father I no longer wanted him to manage me," Janet said. "It would have been easier to have Mother tell him for me, but that was something I had to do for myself. I couldn't say the words—I was bawling like a baby—and finally he just said: 'You don't want me involved in your career. Isn't that it?' 'Yes,' I finally found the nerve to say, 'That's it.'"

The next year, Michael moved out of the mansion as well. He bought a 2,700-acre ranch in Los Olivos, California, for $17 million, and he named it Neverland Valley.

Around the same time, Janet broke with the family religion. Growing up with their staunchly religious Jehovah's Witness mother, Janet and her siblings had been required to attend regular worship services. Katherine took her faith seriously, including the practice of "witnessing," going door-to-door to talk to strangers about her faith and to recruit new members for her church. But when each of her children turned 18, Katherine allowed them to decide for themselves whether following her faith was what they wanted. Michael, LaToya, and Rebbie chose to remain Jehovah's Witnesses. Even as the family's fame grew, Michael would continue the practice of witnessing, at times donning disguises to avoid being recognized. But Janet remembered one of the few times she accompanied her mother on such a trip. She was appalled at how inhospitable many people had been, and she hated the experience.

Later LaToya and then Michael fell out of favor with the church and turned away from it. In her biography, LaToya says she was expelled from the church after she stopped attending regular services. She claimed that she had done so after a friend of hers had been ousted for asking what the church leaders believed was the wrong kind of questions.

Following LaToya's departure from the church, Michael was told not to talk to his sister, a practice meant to instruct those who had "fallen" but which some believe is a punishment. Michael had already been taken to task by church leaders for some of the "occult" images and references in *Thriller*—werewolves, witches, and demons. He chose his relationship with LaToya over the church.

Although she too rejected the family religion, Janet didn't abandon her belief in God. "I was never pushed into the religion by my mother or anyone else," Janet said. "I made up my own mind when I was old enough. I am not a religious person, but I am spiritual. But I don't believe in things like guilt. I believe in a higher power. I believe in inspiration."

5

REVEALING JANET

———— ❦ ————

WITH *CONTROL*, JANET announced to the world that she was all grown up and ready to take the reins in her life. Her next album would tell the world that she cared, that she had a social conscience. But she now felt the added pressure of maintaining the success she had already achieved.

"It was a goal to sell millions of records, and we reached it," Janet said about *Control*. "I was so excited. Now everybody was saying, 'Oh, she did it, but can she do it again?' They said, 'She's just going to be a flash in the pan.' But I knew what I felt. I knew what I had inside me. The thing was to get it out and do it again," Janet said. "A lot of people said, 'Ah, she's just running off her brother's success and it's not going to happen again.' That just fueled the fire. It made me try even harder just to prove them wrong."

Although executives at Janet's label, A&M Records, had specific ideas about how she should follow up on the success of *Control*, Janet already had her own concept in mind, and she refused to adapt it to conform to "marketable" standards. *Rhythm Nation 1814*, released in 1989, showed a new side of Janet. (The date in the title refers to the year in which Francis Scott Key wrote "The Star-Spangled Banner," which became America's national anthem.)

Once again Janet traveled to Minneapolis to collaborate with Harris and Lewis. This time, however,

The phenomenal success of Janet's fourth album, Rhythm Nation 1814, *revealed to the music world a young woman who had hit the top of her profession and was determined to stay there.*

she not only created the concept for the songs but also cowrote six of them with Rene. Janet's songs are about changing the world's problems, but she insists that she wasn't naively believing that she had produced an instruction manual for creating a better world. "No one likes to sit and listen to someone preach for hours and hours," Janet said. "Kids who listen to my music hop from party to party, just having a good time. They pull out the lyric sheet because they're so much into the music, and they come up to me and say, 'Man, I didn't know that song was so serious.' That makes me feel really good."

After she finished recording the album, Janet returned to California to start work on music videos for individual songs. The long hours and fast-paced schedule took their toll on the singer, however. Combined with the strict diet she was following, the routine made Janet feel so weak that one day she collapsed on the set and ended up in a hospital for a few days.

Now that she had two hit records, Janet Jackson would need all of her strength for her first national tour. She had decided that her stage performances would center around her and her dancers, who would act as "soldiers" in a kind of army of reformers. Her outfit was a dark, buttoned-up uniform, and she moved in tight formation with her dancers, a "fighting unit" taking on the world's social ills.

The tour, which lasted about a year, was grueling for Janet and her crew, yet it was a spectacular show. The stage itself soared five stories high and cost $2 million to create. Janet was accompanied onstage by six dancers, pyrotechnics (fireworks), and even a live panther. The premiere show, held in Miami, Florida, didn't go so well, though: "Everything went wrong that night," Janet said. "Everything. The cat! he peed on the stage! I slipped in it. The other dancers slipped in it [too]." But despite its rocky beginning, the show eventually got over its rough spots and was very well-received. "[Janet Jackson's] show combines sleek high-tech and smooth dance rhythm into an evening of snazzy soul with a social conscience," wrote J. Cocks and E. L. Bland in *Time* magazine.

To keep herself in top physical condition and avoid a repeat of the exhaustion she suffered while filming music videos, Janet hired a massage therapist and a chef to accompany her on the luxury bus that traveled from city to city. After checking into a local hotel early each morning, Janet spent the rest of the morning resting before she hit the stage by mid-afternoon for pre-show rehearsals and sound checks. By evening, her makeup and costumes were ready, and Janet burst onto the stage each night with renewed energy. Afterwards, she was back on the bus and headed for another city and another busy day.

Janet's hard work paid off. *Rhythm Nation* dominated the charts with seven Top Five singles and four number-one hits. The record sold 8 million copies and stayed at number one on *Billboard* magazine's Top 200 for four consecutive weeks. Janet Jackson became the first recording artist in music history to land this many top-five songs on the chart from a single album. It was her year to shine: in 1990, she also earned two American Music Awards, and her star was placed on the Hollywood Walk of Fame. When sales statistics from both *Control* and *Rhythm Nation* were added together, Janet had created 12 top-five hits, surpassing even her famous brother's record of 10 from his two wildly popular albums, *Thriller* and *Bad*. Clearly, in a pop music climate of one-hit wonders, Janet had proved that she could not only put out power-packed songs but also that she could keep on doing it consistently.

Part of the appeal of Janet's music at the time was its dance beat, which drew crowds in an era in which discos and dance clubs reigned supreme. "Moves are as vital as music right now. Not since the days of Travolta's white suit [in the smash hit movie *Saturday*

Accompanied by her backup dancers, Janet combined a unique dance beat with her high-powered social-conscience songs. Her concerts garnered rave reviews for her style and energy and drew an ever-growing base of loyal fans.

Night Fever] have the dance floors and the chart tops been so closely aligned," writers for *Time* magazine said. Janet was compared to "dance divas" like Madonna and Paula Abdul as artists who managed to incorporate "strutting their stuff" with musical talent.

By 1991, with high record sales and a growing fan base, Janet had clearly become a top moneymaker in her field. As a result, when her contract with A&M was about to expire, Virgin Records jumped at the opportunity to steal her away. A United Kingdom–based company, Virgin had set up shop in the United States in 1987, and had quickly earned a reputation for finding sizzling talent and promoting it well.

Virgin offered Janet a sweet deal: $50 to $60 million for just two albums, with Virgin having an option to demand additional work. Janet would also get royalties or a percentage of the profit, whichever was greater. Virgin also agreed to pay a substantial part of her video production costs. Very few artists could snag such lucrative recording contracts, and Janet knew it. After her contract with A&M expired in 1993, she signed on with Virgin.

She would not begin working for Virgin Records right away, though. After producing two very successful records, *Control* and *Rhythm Nation 1814*, Janet was ready for a change. She decided to try acting again, but this time she wanted to show what she could do on the big screen, rather than on television. "When [the *Rhythm Nation* concert tour] was over, I thought long and hard about what I wanted to do next," Janet said. "Acting, like singing and dancing, has always stirred my soul, and now was the time to take acting seriously." Finding the right role, however, was tough. "Look at this," Janet said, opening a closet piled with scripts. "None of them moved me. Not one of them seemed right. They were either too slick, too silly, [or] too violent."

Then John Singleton, a young black director whose first big movie was the 1991 hit *Boyz N the Hood*, approached Janet with an unusual script titled *Poetic Justice*. "I immediately loved it," Janet said. "Later, [Singleton] said the part of Justice was written with me in mind, and I was flattered." Singleton had begun writing the script before he met Janet, but at a dinner party with Rene and Janet, he realized that she had a considerable talent for acting. "Janet was telling a story about how these four girls approached her one time," Rene recalled. "Three of them were really nice, saying they like her music. But one of them—there's always one—was saying how she ain't all that, she ain't all that, meaning Janet wasn't such a big deal."

John was surprised to hear Janet deftly slip into street slang to imitate the girl. He began writing the role of Justice—a student who abandons her college plans after her boyfriend is murdered and then turns to poetry to cope with the loss—with Janet in mind.

"I was warned by powerful forces in Hollywood that an all-black movie was the wrong move," Janet said. "Conventional wisdom said I should make a musical. Go for the mainstream white market. Play it safe. John had the same feelings I did—do something different. Then when I accepted the role, other voices started asking, 'How can a rich girl from the 'burbs play a homegirl from the hood?' My reaction was 'Well, watch me.' Besides, isn't acting about entering the soul of someone else?" Janet accepted Singleton's advice to try acting and his offer to appear in his movie.

Poetic Justice focuses on Justice, a hairdresser from South Central Los Angeles whose boyfriend has been gunned down. As a result, she closes herself off from close relationships and consoles herself with the poetry of Maya Angelou. Critics were skeptical of Janet's ability to play a character whose life was so unlike her own, but she defended herself by explaining that Justice's life was not very different from the lives of many of her school friends. "The more I heard the argument, the more determined I became to play the part," she said. "Because I come from a wealthy family doesn't mean I can't relate to a working girl's pain."

Janet eagerly immersed herself in Justice's culture. She even took a job as a hairdresser for a time, walked through the neighborhoods and malls where Justice might have lived, and watched and listened. She invited a fellow hairdresser from South Central to live with her for several weeks so that she could become familiar with the woman's diction and gestures. "They're introverted and complicated and absolutely wonderful people," Janet said of the

Eager to make a film and prove she had serious acting talent, Janet rejected the idea of appearing in a musical. Instead, she accepted an offer from John Singleton, director of the 1991 hit Boyz N the Hood, *to appear in his new film,* Poetic Justice.

women she met in South Central. "In the beginning of the story, Justice is hard-shelled, too. I learned to understand and appreciate that style."

When it was released in 1993, *Poetic Justice* debuted at number one and sold more than 13 million tickets its first weekend, but critics' reviews were decidedly negative. Within just a few weeks, box office sales had dwindled to virtually nothing, and *Poetic Justice* was withdrawn from theaters.

The movie's financial failure didn't dampen Janet Jackson's appreciation for its subject matter. The lessons she learned from her film debut would be incorporated into the lyrics and music of her next album. Making *Poetic Justice* opened a new window for Janet into the life of a "homegirl." She developed a

In Poetic Justice, Janet's char-acter, Justice, consoles her friend Lesha (played by Regina King) after they are confronted with shocking violence. Although the film was not a success, the experience inspired her to think about a new album that would express her most personal and intimate thoughts.

lasting appreciation for the poetry of Maya Angelou. And she felt a renewed sense of her own black heritage.

While she was growing up, Janet says, she didn't hear much about black history or her family's ancestry. "I was never taught that we were kings and queens of this beautiful continent. Never!" Janet said. "That's why I credit rap so much for teaching kids to instill pride. They've helped to enlighten the Caucasian kids as well as other races that we were [African kings and queens] before slavery."

Janet says she has never encountered the kind of extreme racial prejudice she has read and heard about. Instead, her experiences have been more subtle. She remembers, for example, a day when she and Rene made a quick stop at a Beverly Hills boutique, and the sales clerks ignored them until one recognized her as a celebrity. "I was so mad," Janet said. "And I [said], 'So now you are going to be all phony with me. But yet, I know you treat my people like this.'"

Janet also believes that because she is a young woman, some people in the music business have often made the mistake of underestimating her. "A lot of people don't want to follow your directions," she says, talking about encounters with employees and colleagues. "The more fame you get, the easier it gets, but still they feel that by being young you don't know what you are talking about. And on top of that, you are a woman and you are black."

How does she deal with this lack of respect? Her solution is to respond pleasantly and with civility. "I feel that you can get more done with a smile and a kind word, and in the end, no one hates the other one," Janet said. "Everybody is still having a great time; work is still getting done." Yet she is not afraid to stand up for herself if she feels that someone has gone too far. "There are times when people really push you and try to walk over you, and I think that's when you have to put your foot down," Janet told *Ebony* magazine in 1993.

Making *Poetic Justice* not only made Janet aware of her African-American background but also left her hungering to create another album—a work that would help her to disperse the cloud of intense thoughts awakened by the movie. "When the movie was complete, I supposed I did want to shed some of Justice's physical frustration," she told *Rolling Stone* in 1993. "*Rhythm Nation* was a heavy record, and *Poetic Justice* was a heavy movie. I wanted to do something lighter but also daring. Mostly, though, I wanted to do something that corresponded to my life."

The resulting album, *janet,* released that May, would be called the artist's most personal and most intimate. Just as the name suggests, the music, Janet said, was about herself, especially, about how she felt about sex and love.

Janet felt something breaking loose in her after doing *Poetic Justice.* "The film changed me a great deal," Janet said. "It opened me up more, in that sense, to not being as shy [about physical things]. . . . We were so sheltered growing up, and our parents were really strict. So it was the first time I got a chance to see what it's really like out there."

The theme of her new album, Janet said, reflected "a woman who finally feels good enough about her sexuality to demand a man's respect. It's insulting to be seen as some object," she explained. "Women want satisfaction. And so do men. But to get it, you must ask for it. Know what you need. Say what you want."

Janet may describe the album's theme as "communication," "intimacy," or "love," but to most critics and some disapproving parents, "sex" is the blaring message. The cover of the album includes a provocative close-up of the artist's well-toned abdomen above unzipped jeans. The photo drew fire from some observers, who claimed it could not have been Janet Jackson because she was not that fit. "That's really silly to me, because I've never shown my stomach before," Janet objected. "I work out six days a week, for an hour and 40 minutes every day. And I go straight from workouts to rehearsals and work out again [there] for six or seven hours. You cannot help but be in shape." Janet says that she wrote most of the lyrics and many of the melodies for *janet* while working out.

The music videos for the album are equally provocative, and Janet also posed for a now-infamous photo for *Rolling Stone* magazine. She appeared on the

September 16, 1993, cover topless, with Rene's hands cupping her breasts from behind. Still, Janet is adamant that while sexuality permeates the album, the songs are also about becoming a whole person and knowing who you are.

"You see," Janet said, "sex isn't just fire and heat, it's natural beauty. . . . In the age of AIDS, it certainly requires being responsible," she adds. "[But] on a psychological level . . . [it] is also linked with losing yourself . . . using your body to get out of your body. Well, for the first time, I'm feeling free. . . . For me, sex has become a celebration, a joyful part of the creative process."

Several observers have noted that, although *janet* is explicit about sex, it also conveys an innocence and sensitivity. One scholar noted at the time that "Janet's unique persona combines bold, brash power with quiet sensitivity and womanly mystery. Her latest music is lightning and moonglow." Other observers, though, accused her of hitching a ride on the sex-peddling wagon just to sell records.

To make the album, Janet spent hours culling riffs and snippets of melodies and lyrics for inspiration. As a result, she ended up with an eclectic sound—touches of R&B, hip-hop, soul, funk, rock, jazz, and opera that one reviewer called "ambitious" and "flexible" with a "bold impression."

In October 1993 Janet kicked off a worldwide concert tour to promote *janet*. Before she launched the tour, however, she put in some heavy practice time. Janet "turns into a conscientious student dead set on mastering the meticulous routines," wrote *Rolling Stone* at the time. She was "giggling at the miscues, going along with jokes about her shapely backside, kidding her partners about their love lives. In black sweat pants, baggy Mickey Mouse T-shirt and baseball cap with 'Funky Essentials' scrawled across the crown, she looks 17, not 27."

By the time the show was ready for the road, Janet

Sweatpants, a Micky Mouse T-shirt, and a turned-around baseball cap revealed a funky, playful Janet when she performed at the 1993 MTV Awards.

and her dance group had nailed every move. With a closet full of halter tops and tights—Janet's stage costumes—an ornate Spanish-style set, and a well-rehearsed crew, the show premiered. And, despite all the talk of her new album's in-your-face sexuality, Janet's tour was much less raucous than those of colleagues such as Madonna. "Next to Madonna's Blond Ambition tour, Jackson's hip-grinding innuendo was strictly PG," a reviewer noted in 1994.

Janet Jackson's new album reached number one and stayed there for six weeks in 1993. It also spawned a slew of single hits. "That's the Way Love Goes" spent eight weeks at number one and went platinum (meaning that it sold a million copies). "You Want This" was a Top 10 song and her 15th single to reach gold, setting a new record for Janet, who had earned more gold singles than any other female singer. For Janet, success couldn't have sounded any sweeter.

6

EASING HER BURDENS

❦

A S JANET'S CAREER skyrocketed, it became increasingly important that she have a comfortable home of her own, where she felt free both to relax and to work. She finally found it in a beachfront house in Malibu, California, along the Pacific Coast Highway. There she loves to listen to waves crashing on the shore and watch sunsets from the privacy of her own balcony.

Janet has decorated her home with a broad array of objects that reflect her travels and her interests. The foyer is filled with lush plants and sculptures, and is guarded by a wall-to-ceiling framed shark fossil. The living room, large enough to accommodate 200 people, is dotted with African art and accented with seashells and live cacti. One wall is painted to match the ocean view, sky-blue above and deep blue below. Janet's kitchen is high-tech; she has hired a chef who creates low-fat, healthy, and meatless meals for her. Lining the hallway leading to Janet's private gym is a series of black-and-white photographs of her with Rene. Inside the gym, a massive stereo system pounds out lively music whenever Janet is working out.

David Ritz of *Rolling Stone*, who interviewed Janet in her home in 1993, described it as peaceful and Janet herself as serene: "She wore a long linen dress in earth tones with a low scooped neck. Her

At ease in the peace and comfort of her home, Janet finds the happiness and contentment she needs to help her relax from the burdens of her incredible success.

feet were bare, as was her face. She wore no jewelry. She snacked on a slice of whole wheat, unbuttered bread. An ocean breeze, pounding surf, and squawking sea gulls overcame her soft voice, making it almost impossible to hear her."

During the interview, Rene affectionately ran his hand along Janet's back as her fingers slid into his hand. "He's so incredibly supportive," she said of Rene. "We're all human, we go through things. [The relationship involves] a lot of give and take. You can't run the moment that a problem comes about. You have to work it out." Rene's supportiveness included his involvement in Janet's career; he helped her work on dance steps and the lyrics and music of her songs as well as providing an emotional brace. She continued:

> I've been very fortunate to have found someone who has been so incredibly caring. . . . I don't think anybody else would have stuck around because [I had some] really difficult time[s]. . . . And I know he probably would wake up and say, "Okay, who is she today?" I think anyone else would have said, "You know what? I am out of here because I cannot take this." But he was there, right by my side the entire way.

Like many other artists, Janet often finds elements of her career and her music in nearly everything she sees and does. Both she and her brother Michael have reputations in the music industry as extremely hard workers. They are willing to put into their careers as much time and energy as is necessary to make their music the best it can be. But Janet does relax occasionally. When an interviewer accused her of being too serious, Janet seemed surprised. "Gosh, no! I can be silly," she replied. "I often am. I believe in work, work, work, but also play, play, play. Like everyone else, I read . . . novels and go out to the movies."

Janet holds the Sammy Davis Jr. Award she received in 1992. With all her awards and accolades, however, Janet still has to contend with her self-image. She has been struggling with a weight problem for many years. But mindful of the dangers of extreme dieting and with the same determination she brings to her work, Janet keeps her figure slim and toned in a healthy way.

Janet also spends free time with friends, many of whom are members of her dance troupe, the Kids. She's been known to hop in her Jeep and drive one of them to a class or take a few of them to lunch. She also enjoys dancing at nightclubs. For a long vacation, Janet recently headed to the West Indies, where she soaked up the tropical sun and the island music.

One of the issues that Janet has a difficult time relaxing about is her weight. For her, it has always been an issue. From childhood on, Janet struggled with a mild weight problem. When she was a young

Two years before her death from heart failure because of obsessive dieting, an emaciated Karen Carpenter appears with her brother, Richard (left), and A&M Records' president Herb Alpert at a reception honoring the Carpenters' more than 12 years as recording artists.

girl performing with her family, her siblings and parents sometimes teased her about being "pudgy." As a result, Janet became more and more concerned about her figure as she grew into a teenager.

In show business, the pressure to have a "perfect body" can be overwhelming. For women, it's enough to cause an obsession—and in some cases, it can prove deadly. In 1983, Karen Carpenter, part of the brother-sister pop duo known as the Carpenters, died of heart failure brought on by anorexia nervosa. At her death, Karen, who was only 32 years old, weighed just 75 pounds. Twenty years earlier, Dinah Washington died after mixing alcohol with the diet pills to which she had become addicted. She too weighed a scant 75 pounds.

Janet was familiar with the environment that led these women to develop eating disorders. "Men can be chubby, woman can't," Janet says of people's expectations. "It's a hell of a price. Who's to say what perfect is? We women beat ourselves up a great deal, and there's no need for that." When she was heavy, Janet said, people treated her with disdain at times. "People look at you differently, as if you're not human," Janet said. "And that's what people have to understand—you are human; you have struggles and problems and obstacles, maybe on a broader scale because you're in the public eye and there are certain demands on you."

When she was in her early teens, Janet, who is now a vegetarian, decided that she needed to lose weight. "The problem is, I like food," Janet said at the time. "I like Italian, French, and good old McDonald's fries. . . . I know I need to lose weight," she said with a resigned sigh. "I'm good at starting my diet tomorrow. . . . Of course, if I gain too many extra pounds, there's always someone around to tell me and then I have to do something about it." Finally, in 1988, after *Rhythm Nation* was released, Janet slimmed down for good.

During the *Rhythm Nation* tour Janet became so concerned over a little extra weight she'd gained that she added more workouts to her exercise routine and cut her calorie intake drastically. At one point she became so exhausted that she had to cancel a couple of performances. "I began to realize that whenever something really painful was going on, I would eat, and that's how I would run away from it," Janet said. "But [by overdoing dieting] I would just be creating another problem in another area instead of just dealing with that pain."

Instead Janet decided to shape up in a healthy way. She began a balanced diet and exercise plan. She ate mostly broiled fish and vegetables, practiced her dance routines for six hours a day, lifted weights, and did hundreds of abdominal crunches. By the time she launched the *janet* tour, she was taut and sinewy at 110 pounds.

Despite more than a decade of being slim and toned, Janet says she still struggles with her body image. "I remember someone asked me to pick out something that I like about my [body]," Janet said recently. "So I'm sitting there and I'm going, 'I like the small of my back. I like my ankles, I like my eyes and my teeth. . . .' Liking me overall? I'm still working on that one."

Aside from her weight, one of the greatest struggles in Janet's life concerns her family. Even as an adult, Janet deals with discord among her siblings and her difficult relationships with her parents. Most of the blame, according to several of the Jackson children, goes to their father, Joseph. "From the beginning Joseph was a strict father who would not hesitate to strike his children if he felt they deserved to be punished," Bart Andrews claimed in his 1994 biography of Janet. The author says that Joseph Jackson attributes his approach to the fact that he himself was physically punished while growing up. "I got whippings all the time," Joseph has reportedly said. Publicly, however, the Jacksons appeared to be the perfect family. The children were polite, and the family seemed quite close-knit. Michael, LaToya, and Janet even chose to live with their parents after graduating from high school.

The first clue that the picture-perfect Jackson family wasn't what it seemed came in 1988, with the publication of Michael's autobiography, *Moonwalk*. In it Michael accused his father of physically abusing him. "If you messed up during rehearsal, you got hit," Michael remembered. "Sometimes with a belt. Sometimes with a switch." He remembered one time when he didn't execute a dance step perfectly and Joseph smacked him across the face so

hard that he fell backward. "But I'd also get beaten for things that happened outside rehearsal," wrote Michael.

During a 1992 interview with Oprah Winfrey, Michael revealed that he was so afraid of his father as a child that he would sometimes "regurgitate" if Joseph came near. Joseph remained unrepentant; when he was interviewed after Michael's appearance, Joseph said, "If he did gurgitate, he gurgitated all the way to the bank. But me being strict with

Michael Jackson gives talk show host Oprah Winfrey a tour of his ranch in California. In 1988, Michael wrote of the less than perfect family life of the Jacksons, claiming beatings and abuse by his father. In a later interview with Oprah, Michael revealed how much he feared his father.

him a little bit, it made him a superstar. Look, he didn't just happen on his own. He had to have a beginning. All of them had to have a beginning."

In her own 1991 autobiography, LaToya also accused her father of physically abusing her and her mother of refusing to intervene. Janet, however, denied that Joseph had been anything but strict with his children. "Mike was wrong to say he was physically abused," Janet said after *Moonwalk* came out. "That's not really true. He was whooped, but not abused. People just don't get it. African Americans use the word beat, but that's not always what they mean. I have black girlfriends who will say to me, 'We got whooped as kids,' but they don't mean beat up."

Janet remembered Joseph as stern but fair. And she was quick to remind people that Joseph had raised very successful children. "Who knows what would have happened to my brothers if they had been allowed to roam around the streets?" Janet said. "Who knows what would have happened to LaToya and Rebbie? The streets were dangerous. I always say my parents made the best choices they could at the time. I believe that with all my heart," she insists in Andrews's biography.

Although in public Janet has been vague about the emotional effects of her father's distance and disapproval, close observers claim that she was devastated by it. "Watching her forge the music over many months, I saw something I hadn't seen before—how much Janet suffers from a past that's alarmingly clear and frustratingly vague," wrote David Ritz in *Rolling Stone*. "I wanted to ask Janet the same thing I had wanted to ask Jermaine, Tito, Jackie, Randy, and Michael: What the hell happened to you guys? What kind of mangled childhood makes you so . . . nice, yet so ill-equipped to talk about what the niceness is covering? But their niceness kept me from asking, even as I knew Janet was the only one who seemed to be struggling for an answer."

As the youngest child, Janet may have come closer than any of the Jackson children to winning her father's affection. "He wasn't easy to warm up to, and I don't know that any of us really knew him," Janet said. "But I loved him. And I believed he loved us. I do believe that. I was closest to him, I think. I tried to be, anyway. But there was a sadness about him."

Joseph's alleged abuse hasn't been the only problem for the Jackson family. LaToya sparked a great family uproar in 1989 when she posed nude for *Playboy* magazine. Jermaine and Jackie both ended their marriages in divorce. Joseph himself continued to philander, and his relationship with Katherine crumbled. Jermaine released a song called "Word to the Badd" that contained lyrics criticizing his younger brother Michael.

Janet herself became the target of hurtful accusations when LaToya, in her autobiography, accused her younger sister of anti-Semitism, insisted that Janet was extremely jealous of Michael's success, and described her as treacherous and deceptive. Janet did not take the accusations lightly. Not until six years later, in the fall of 1997, did the two begin repairing their relationship.

Meanwhile, Michael Jackson was under fire himself. He'd long been criticized for his eccentric behavior, his reclusiveness, and his numerous facial plastic surgeries. He also was taken to task for supposedly trying to lighten his skin, although his changing skin tone was later attributed to a rare medical condition. But in August of 1993, Michael was accused of molesting a 13-year-old boy. Police raided his homes and the Jackson family mansion in an attempt to find out what really happened.

The accusations raised questions about the good deeds Michael had been doing for children, including

Janet and her sister LaToya (left) were estranged for several years when, in her autobiography, LaToya, like Michael, claimed physical abuse by her father; she also accused Janet of treachery, deception, and jealousy. Janet has strenuously denied both her siblings' claims, explaining that her father was strict but fair.

bringing poor and sick children to his ranch for fantasy vacations. The accusations were never proven, and Michael insisted they were part of an extortion attempt.

While many members of her family rushed to support Michael publicly, Janet held back. She had firmly believed for some time that the best way to deal with scandal is to refuse to respond to it, to drop a wall of silence. "The best thing we can do as a family," Janet has said, "is to keep our traps shut."

Janet remains fiercely loyal to her family, but there is a part of her that wishes to separate from her famous siblings. During one interview with *Rolling Stone*, she even talked about changing her last name. "If I do it, I'll do it quietly," Janet said. "I wouldn't make a big announcement, and I wouldn't want my family to think I'm ashamed of them. I'm not; I love them. But . . . I've always wanted to be just Janet. I've always wanted to simplify and feel like I'm standing on my own."

Janet's next project would prove not only that she was a talented performer in her own right, but also that she had learned to transcend the difficulties with her family and strike out on her own emotional journey.

7

ANOTHER EVOLUTION

❧

Much of Janet's success has been her chameleonlike ability to evolve as a performer and reinvent herself. At a 1995 concert in London, fans had the opportunity to see and hear yet another incarnation—a hip, trendy, new-age entertainer.

In 1996, AFTER the successful release of *janet*, Virgin Records lobbied to keep Janet on their label by negotiating a new, $80-million, four-album contract that gave her an unprecedented 24 percent of royalties from the sale of the forthcoming albums. The deal was the envy of recording artists everywhere.

So what would Janet do this time? Even for an entertainer who was known for her ability to recreate herself with each new project, the album she created was yet another surprise. Those working on the project were no strangers to her, however; Harris and Lewis wrote the music and produced the album, and Rene received credit for his input.

The music of *The Velvet Rope* is complicated, and the lyrics are sometimes explicit. The album was a risk and Janet knew it. Some took issue with the title, believing the album was about bondage. There were those who thought that some of Janet's lyrics suggested that she was "coming out" as a homosexual or a bisexual. Others criticized her because they felt that she was simply trying to be raunchy to sell records. The truth, Janet once again insisted, was that she was using her music to expose her inner life—who she was and what she thought and cared about. And the self she exposed was complex and multifaceted.

One reviewer called Janet a "realistic chameleon

Janet performs in Washington, D.C., on her Velvet Rope tour. Along with her new look, which included tatoos and body piercings, Janet created a new theme. She wanted, she said, to reveal her inner self and inspire the audience to experience what she was feeling.

we love to anticipate because we never quite know exactly how she's going to present herself. Plus, she rarely disappoints us." The album was "honest, wise" with "messages of hope, guidance, sexual liberation and unconditional love, whatever one's sexual preference."

Here's a sampling of what the album offers: a song about having everything except genuine happiness, another about a physically abusive relationship, one about discrimination, another about friends who have died of AIDS, yet another about the pain caused by homophobia. But even with its explicit and sometimes sexually ambiguous lyrics, many critics agreed that *The Velvet Rope* was much more about love than about sex. *Entertainment Weekly* wrote:

> Mostly . . . it's Jackson's delivery that keeps the album out of the gutter. Rather than stress the nudge-wink naughtiness of the lyric, Jackson would rather sing about sex as if it were simply a fact of life. . . . In fact, it's the emotional component of sex, rather than the act itself, that seems Jackson's real concern. That's one of the reasons it's a mistake to judge this album on the basis of its lyric sheet. . . . The most revealing moments here have to do with loneliness and vulnerability, not sexual preference.

Janet agrees that the primary message in her work is self-disclosure. In the two or three years before the album came out, Janet says she began to struggle with depression. The songs on *The Velvet Rope* were her way of exploring and coming to terms with the pain that had caused her depression.

Between 1995 and 1997, Janet says the depression intensified. "There were times when I felt very hopeless and helpless, and I felt like walls were kind of closing in on me. . . . But I didn't know what it was and it would come, like, here and there. I thought I was just having a funky day. And it just got progressively worse until it was every day." Finally, a year or so before she began recording *The Velvet Rope,* Janet decided to stop running from her feelings. She hoped that by dealing with them in her own way—which would mean making them part of her music—she could begin to feel better about herself.

"Singing these songs has meant digging up pain that I buried a long time ago," she said. "It's been hard and sometimes confusing. But I've had to do it. I've been burying pain my whole life. It's like kicking dirt under the carpet. At some point there's so much dirt you start to choke. Well, I've been choking. . . . My therapy came in writing these songs. Then I had to find the courage to sing them or else suffer the consequences—a permanent case of [depression]."

Some of Janet's pain, she said, arose from her childhood and her father's indifference; some came from her failed marriage and from her siblings' struggles. And this is probably the key to Janet's rapport with her fans—her willingness, even eagerness, to share intimate thoughts and feelings with them.

Despite Janet's noble intentions, however, *The Velvet Rope* was less successful than her previous records had been. Though it debuted at number one on *Billboard*'s Top 200 list, it fell off a week later and stayed in the Top 10 for just three weeks. Janet was privately disappointed, but in public she stood firm against critics. "I'm not patting myself on the back," Janet said. "But showing your true self means leaving yourself open for people to take shots at you."

By and large, the album's music—and Janet herself—was strong enough to weather the criticism. As a review in *Rolling Stone* said, "Pared down, *The Velvet Rope* would have brushed up against brilliance. Still, it's a testimonial to the record's merits that it's ultimately stronger than Jackson's sense of self-importance."

In September 1997 Janet launched a year-long Velvet Rope tour, ultimately playing to 33 sold-out audiences in Europe and to nearly half a million fans altogether. In the United States she broke house records in Washington, D.C.; Grand Rapids and Detroit, Michigan; and Salt Lake City, Utah. And as Janet sang, album sales surged, so that by the fall of 1998 *The Velvet Rope* had sold nearly 5.5 million copies.

Janet had prepared for the personal appearances by cultivating a new look—fit and pierced. She increased the intensity of her workouts and slimmed down a bit. To keep up with the grueling concert schedule, Janet brought her chef, choreographer, exercise trainer, and massage therapist along. Doug

A crowd of fans strain to touch and photograph Janet as she appears at a New York City music store for a CD signing of her recording The Velvet Rope.

Yee, Janet's trainer, said that even while touring, Janet worked hard to keep fit. "Most people would not like to go through the workout she does," he said. "If one is couch potato and ten is triathlete, when she's on tour I'd put Janet around an eight in terms of her fitness level."

Janet's massage therapist also helped her relax by administering what is called Amma Therapy. For example, the therapist would light a "moxa stick," which looks like a cigar, next to Janet's ankles. The heat supposedly energized the kidneys and spleen and gave the star a jump start. Janet also meditated each morning and evening. Then, every so often, the whole crew would take a week off to unwind.

As for the piercings, Janet has had several, including her tongue and nose. "It was something I wanted to do," she says. "It's pain with artistic results. The tattoos are tribal. The logo for *The Velvet Rope*, tattooed on the inside of my wrist, is African in origin. Its meaning is roughly, 'Explore your past to build your future.' . . . I've always wanted to do these things but was afraid of displeasing people. Now I'm just flat-out pleasing myself."

Along with choosing a new look, Janet also chose a fresh new theme for the concert. "It's the first time I've directed a show by myself," Janet said. "I saw it as a landscape of my inner self. I wanted the crowd to feel what I'm feeling. I mapped it out—here's when I want them to feel anger, here's when I want them to get down and get funky, here's when I want them to feel the pain. . . . Finally I had to follow my instincts about representing myself as honestly as possible. That's why the show starts with one of my dancers opening a giant scrapbook. . . . The show is an open book [about my life]."

At a concert stop in Vancouver, Canada, David Ritz caught a glimpse of what life was like for Janet off-stage. "She flops around hotel suites in old jeans and pajama tops," Ritz wrote in *Rolling Stone*. "Without makeup, her face seems more vulnerable. Her eyes are clear and somewhat wistful." On tour with Janet Jackson in Tokyo, Japan, Ritz observed Janet's interaction with fans and the "fishbowl" life of being a world celebrity:

> The crowd in Shibuya, an urban zone of sleek vertical malls, verges on a mob scene. The fashion is edgy, and the average fan looks no older than eighteen. . . . [Janet] sits in a . . . radio studio, visible to all.
>
> I watch hundreds of fans watching Janet Jackson watching them. They are teenagers, mostly girls, many of them crying. Their noses press against the glass. When Janet waves or nods, they openly sob. Their hands shake. When Janet answers a simple question— "Are you happy to be here?"—with a simple "Yes," her whisper-quiet voice provokes screams.
>
> There's a certain anguish in Janet's voice and the reactions of her fans, an unspoken dialogue that I don't entirely get. Two Japanese girls hold a sign that reads, "Janet. Please see us. Please understand." Afterward, I ask them through a translator what it is they want understood. "She already understands," they say. "What?" I want to know. "Us," they reply. The girls are fourteen, maybe fifteen.

So, did it work? Did making an album about private pain alleviate Janet's depression? In some ways, Janet says, yes. "I never looked deeply at the pain from my past, never tried to understand that pain and work through it," Janet said. Although she feels she has made progress, she describes her quest for happiness as "a journey that I'm still walking."

One of the reasons Janet has managed to achieve worldwide fame and remain popular despite all of her changes is that, in spite of her soft voice and perpetual niceness, she's competitive at her core. "That's how we were raised, really," Janet said. "It comes from my father as well as my mother." Janet's parents encouraged their children to compete with each other. When it comes to Michael, however, competing is an uphill battle. His *Thriller* album is still the biggest seller of all time, with a total of more than 110 million copies sold. "It is a friendly competition because he is my brother," Janet said. "If it were somebody else, I'd still want to break the record. We talk on the phone all the time, and he knows I want to break his records. But I'm really proud of him. And I really look up to him. He inspires me a great deal."

Even after years on her own, Janet still fears that she doesn't measure up to her brother, yet at times she tires of the questioning from critics who constantly compare her to Michael. "I keep imagining that everyone is looking at me, thinking, 'She doesn't dance as well as Michael,' or 'Her videos are not as exciting as Michael's,' or 'Is she going to be as successful as Michael?'" Janet says. "They expect so much and I get very tired of it."

Proof that the contest between the siblings is friendly came in 1995, when Janet costarred with Michael on the first single from his comeback album, *HIStory*. The music video of the song, titled "Scream," featured the siblings dressed in silver and white clothing, roaming the spooky corridors of an empty spaceship and playing the 1970s video game "Pong" on a giant video screen. The song reached number five on the Top 100 chart.

As for competition with other artists, Janet doesn't feel quite the same intense drive. Among the artists in her league are Whitney Houston, Madonna, and Mariah Carey. Janet is not known for her powerful or versatile voice, as Houston is, so she had to work hard to make sure her entire presentation packs a wallop. "She may have the weakest singing voice of her

superstar contemporaries Whitney, Mariah, and Toni [Braxton], but gorgeous, classy Jackson is still one of the most innovative, nonbandwagon jumping, best selling album makers of her time," wrote Vince Aletti in September 1997 in the *Village Voice*.

Janet says she greatly admires Whitney Houston, and especially loves her powerful voice. On the other hand, Janet doesn't have much respect for Madonna. She has said that Madonna can neither sing nor dance, but relies on exhibitionism to sell records. Janet makes no apologies for her competitive streak, though. It has, after all, brought her a long way. "If someone is at number one and I'm at number two,

Teaming up with Michael, Janet appeared in his fantasy music video of the single "Scream" from his album, HIStory. Although close to Michael, Janet's competitive spirit spurs her to try and break her brother's record in reaching the top of the pop music charts.

then I want the number-one spot," Janet said. "But I feel there is enough room for everyone."

So what's next for this woman who at 33 years old seems to have everything? Janet says she wants to pursue acting again; indeed, in October 1999 she began filming a sequel to the 1996 comedy *The Nutty Professor*, starring Eddie Murphy. She has also been interested in bringing the stories of the actresses she most admires to the screen, such as Dorothy Dandridge, a beautiful African-American actress who in the 1950s starred in films like *Carmen Jones* and *Porgy and Bess*. Dandridge died of a sleeping pill overdose in 1965. So far nothing has come of this interest, but Janet talks about the project every now and then.

Janet also has to complete three more albums to fulfill her contract obligations to Virgin Records. With the broad range of music she's created thus far, it will be interesting to see the shape-shifting Janet does next time, as well the subjects she will choose. "The thing that excites me isn't becoming a bigger star but a better artist, deeper, truer to the things I find exciting," Janet said. "I hope to be an honest artist—no more, no less."

As far as her private life, Janet is noncommittal. In 1998, rumors circulated that she and Rene had been married for years; the story began with Janet's sister Rebbie, who announced it during a radio interview promoting her own album. Yet Janet and Rene claimed that they were simply living together. And though they appeared to be very much in love, Janet wasn't eager to make their union legal and seemed almost suspicious about taking that step. "We like it the way it is," Janet said at the time. "We feel like we're spiritually connected. When someone in the public eye gets married, there's a feeling of . . . putting this negative energy in the air. . . . A friend said, 'Why don't you get a tattoo of Rene's initials?' I go, 'No, I will never.'

The minute I do, we'll break up, and I won't be able to get rid of that." But did she want to spend the rest of her life with Rene? She sighed, "I'd love nothing more."

Unfortunately, that seems to be a dream that will not come true. In February 1999, Janet's publicist announced that the couple had split romantically, although they continue to remain close friends.

"Do I want children?" Janet asks aloud. "I'm not sure. When I was a teenager, I wanted 12 kids. Then, as I got older, I wasn't so sure a big family was such a great thing. It's a tough job. . . . [W]hen do you let them fall, when do you pick them up—you know? I have this fear of not being a good enough parent. I know there's no such thing as the perfect parent, but I'd want to be as close to it as possible."

One part of her future about which Janet is certain is her goal to reach the top of the charts the way her brother Michael did. "I always try to give 110 percent to everything I do," she says. Breaking Michael's records is now, more than ever before, a reachable goal for Janet. And she may very well succeed. Michael is now in his forties, which makes it harder for him to relate to—and sell to—teen and young adult audiences. In addition, the public attention and scandals surrounding the star have diminished his appeal.

Many of those who have interviewed or spent time with Janet refer to her as the "normal" Jackson. In a family rocked by controversy and marred by allegations of abuse, Janet seems to have emerged as the healthiest of all the celebrity siblings. "Who really knows why or how Janet Jackson turned out the way she did—a sharp-witted, level headed, usually rational young lady?" biographer Andrews asked. "The fact is, she did, and her inner strength and deep resolve are as much a part of her true personality as Michael's extreme sensitivity and LaToya's extreme fragility are parts of theirs."

On a tour of South Africa in 1998, Janet took time from her busy schedule to visit with youngsters in the SOS Children's Village outside Johannesburg.

Janet alone among the Jacksons has remained a wildly popular, hip entertainer. She has climbed to the top in the music world and may someday make her mark in Hollywood as well. Her family's success provided both a head start and a handicap. Janet Jackson "must feel the heat from rising stars like Mary J. Blige, Toni Braxton, Bjork, Mariah Carey, and Alanis Morissette," wrote Vince Aletti in a 1997 *Village Voice* article, "but Janet cruises in more rarefied air. Like Madonna, and with few other peers, she combines a pure pop sensibility with ambition, vulnerability, freakishness, and extraordinary savvy." Janet is, in her own word, "special," a true contender in the competitive world of pop music, and a traveler on the road to self-awareness and happiness.

CHRONOLOGY

1966	Janet Dameta Jackson born on May 16 in Gary, Indiana, the ninth and last child of Joseph and Katherine Jackson
1968	Tito, Jackie, Jermaine, Marlon, and Michael move with their father, Joseph, to Los Angeles, California, after receiving a recording contract with Berry Gordy; the rest of the family joins them 18 months later
1969	The Jackson Five's first album, *Diana Ross Presents the Jackson Five*, is released
1971	The Jackson family moves into a mansion in Encino, California; a weekly animated series featuring the Jackson Five premieres on television
1974	Janet debuts onstage with the Jackson Five at the MGM Grand Hotel in Las Vegas, Nevada
1977–79	Plays Penny Gordon on the television program *Good Times*
1980	Appears in TV comedy *Diff'rent Strokes*
1981	With her sisters, launches an unsuccessful singing group modeled on the Jackson Five
1982	First album, *Janet Jackson*, is released
1984	Second album, *Dream Street*, is released; begins acting in TV series *Fame*; graduates from high school. Elopes with James DeBarge on September 7
1985	Marriage is annulled in November
1986	*Control*, produced by Jimmy "Jam" Harris and Terry Lewis, is released to wide acclaim; album's first single, "What Have You Done for Me Lately?" reaches number one on the charts. Janet becomes romantically involved with long-time friend Rene Elizondo
1987	Wins two American Music Awards (out of nine nominations) for *Control*; moves out of family home and fires father, Joseph Jackson, as her manager
1988	Michael's autobiography, *Moonwalk*, is published; the book contains allegations of physical abuse in the Jackson family
1989	*Rhythm Nation 1814* is released; Janet launches first national tour
1990	Wins two American Music Awards and is given a star on the Hollywood Walk of Fame

1991	LaToya Jackson publishes autobiography accusing Joseph Jackson of physical abuse and Janet of anti-Semitism and deceptiveness
1993	Signs with new label, Virgin Records; appears in feature film *Poetic Justice*; releases *janet*; launches first worldwide concert tour
1995	Costars with brother Michael in music video of the single "Scream" from his *HIStory* album; releases *Design of a Decade 1986/1996*, a compilation of her hit singles
1996	Negotiates a new, $80 million recording contract with Virgin Records
1997	*The Velvet Rope* is released; Janet announces that a portion of the proceeds from the second single, "Together Again," will be donated to the American Foundation for AIDS (AmFAR); reveals her struggle with depression
1998	"Together Again" nominated for an MTV Video Music Award
1999	Announces her split from Rene Elizondo; begins filming *The Nutty Professor 2* with Eddie Murphy

DISCOGRAPHY AND FILMOGRAPHY

ALBUMS

Janet Jackson (1982)

Dream Street (1984)

Control (1986)

Rhythm Nation 1814 (1989)

janet (1993)

Design of a Decade 1986/1996 (1995)

The Velvet Rope (1997)

TELEVISION

The Jacksons (1976–77)

Good Times (1977–79)

Diff'rent Strokes (1981–82)

The Love Boat (1984, guest appearance)

Fame (1984–85)

Everybody Dance Now (1991, special)

Racism: Points of View (1991, special)

Hollywood's Leading Ladies With David Sheehan (1993, special)

FILM

Poetic Justice (1993)

The Nutty Professor 2 (2000)

Beginning in 1987, when she won two American Music Awards for her album Control, *Janet has continued to receive recognition for her musical artistry. Here, she holds her latest award, given in 1999 by the World Music Awards for her outstanding contribution to rhythm and blues.*

FURTHER READING

Andrews, Bart. *Out of the Madness: The Strictly Unauthorized Biography of Janet Jackson*. New York: HarperPaperbacks, 1994.

Jackson, Katherine, with Richard Wiseman. *My Family, the Jacksons*. New York: St. Martin's Press, 1990.

Jackson, LaToya, with Patricia Romanowski. *Growing Up in the Jackson Family*. New York: Dutton, 1991.

Jackson, Michael. *Moonwalk*. New York: Doubleday, 1988.

Nicholson, Lois P. *Michael Jackson*. New York: Chelsea House Publishers, 1994.

Taraborrelli, Randy. *Michael Jackson: The Magic and the Madness*. New York: Ballantine Books, 1991.

INDEX

PICTURE CREDITS

CINDY DYSON is a former newspaper journalist who is now a full-time freelance writer. Her work has appeared in many national and regional magazines. This is her second book for Chelsea House Publishers.

NATHAN IRVIN HUGGINS, one of America's leading scholars in the field of black studies, helped select the titles for the BLACK AMERICANS OF ACHIEVEMENT series, for which he also served as senior consulting editor. He was the W. E. B. DuBois Professor of History and Afro-American Studies at Harvard University and the director of the W. E. B. DuBois Institute for Afro-American Research at Harvard. He received his doctorate from Harvard in 1962 and returned there as professor in 1980 after teaching at Columbia University, the University of Massachusetts, Lake Forest College, and the California State University, Long Beach. He was the author of four books and dozens of articles, including *Black Odyssey: The Afro-American Ordeal in Slavery*, *The Harlem Renaissance*, and *Slave and Citizen: The Life of Frederick Douglass*, and was associated with the Children's Television Workshop, National Public Radio, the Boston Athenaeum, the Museum of Afro-American History, the Howard Thurman Educational Trust, and Upward Bound. Professor Huggins died in 1989, at the age of 62, in Cambridge, Massachusetts.